THE ORGANIC SUBURBANITE

THE ORGANIC SUBURBANITE

AN ENVIRONMENTALLY FRIENDLY WAY TO LIVE THE AMERICAN DREAM

WARREN SCHULTZ

RODALE

RODALE

WE **INSPIRE** AND **ENABLE** PEOPLE TO IMPROVE
THEIR LIVES AND THE WORLD AROUND THEM

We're always happy to hear from you. For questions or comments concerning the editorial content of this book, please write to:

Rodale Book Readers' Service
33 East Minor Street
Emmaus, PA 18098

Look for other Rodale books wherever books are sold, or call us at (800) 848-4735.

For more information about Rodale Organic Living magazines and books, visit us at
www.organicgardening.com

Editor: Deborah L. Martin
Cover and Interior Book Designer: Marcella Bove-Huttie
Senior Designer: Nancy S. Biltcliff
Cover Photographer: FPG International
Photography Editor: Lyn Horst
Photography Assistant: Jackie L. Ney
Layout Designer: Dale Mack
Researcher: Diana Erney
Copy Editor: Sarah Sacks Dunn
Manufacturing Coordinator: Jodi Schaffer
Indexer: Nan N. Badgett
Editorial Assistance: Kerrie A. Cadden

Rodale Organic Living Books
Executive Editor: Kathleen DeVanna Fish
Managing Editor: Fern Marshall Bradley
Executive Creative Director: Christin Gangi
Art Director: Patricia Field
Production Manager: Robert V. Anderson Jr.
Studio Manager: Leslie M. Keefe
Copy Manager: Nancy N. Bailey

Library of Congress Cataloging-in-Publication Data
Schultz, Warren.
    The organic suburbanite : an environmentally friendly way to live the American dream / Warren Schultz.
        p.   cm.
    Includes bibliographical references and index.
    ISBN 0–87596–860–0 (pbk. : alk. paper)
    1. Organic gardening—United States.   2. Home economics—United States.   3. Human ecology—United States.   I. Title.
    SB453.5 .S556   2001
    635'.0484—dc21   00–011435

Distributed in the book trade by St. Martin's Press

2 4 6 8 10 9 7 5 3 1   paperback

To Susan, for all of those plastic
sandwich bags washed,
hung over the sink to dry,
and reused

Health, Harmony, Organic Style

Dear Reader,

Aren't the best moments in your life the ones where you feel most connected to the best in yourself, in harmony with nature and with the world around you? When you do the right thing for others, yourself, and nature, you can't help but feel happy and at peace.

The choices you make can make your life more joyful. You can choose how to live, eat, travel, raise your family, work, and get in touch with your soul in ways that lead you to a better future and more moments of happiness . . . the moments that really matter.

The best choices for you are often the best choices for nature. Choices that preserve all that you love and need. Choices that help you lead a healthier life. Choices that leave you with a clean conscience and a happy heart.

The great news is that these days, the right choices can be beautiful, delicious, stylish, fun, and deeply satisfying. Let *Organic Style* magazine and books be your guide to doing the right thing and loving every minute of it.

Rodale has brought you the most important and inspiring information on healthy active organic living since 1942. Join us as *Organic Style* continues in this rich tradition.

Welcome to a future you want to live in!

Maria Rodale
Rodale Organic Style Books

Contents

Reinventing Suburbia.

There's a new day dawning in suburbia. Folks who live there are asking themselves how they can make their bedroom communities more environmentally sound. That's a big change from the original intentions that brought the suburbs into existence.

The suburbs weren't built with the environment in mind. No, the suburbs were built for our comfort and convenience. In fact, the creation of these developments demonstrated our domination of nature. To build the suburbs, developers with monstrous machines cleared trees, mowed meadows and prairies, stripped away topsoil, drained marshes, and dammed rivers. And once it was all level and uniform, houses were plunked down—with lots of space between them—and joined together by winding lanes of pavement and oceans of grass.

The suburbs were born during a more innocent time. Natural resources seemed endlessly abundant and there for the taking. It was a guilt-free time, when station wagons roamed the earth. Those were the days when a weekend's entertainment meant going for a drive. It was a time when pesticides represented progress and promised less work and more food.

More than 50 years later, suburban developments are still springing up across the country. We haven't run out of land . . . yet. And although we may be more ecologically aware these days, the suburbs still are not the easiest place to live lightly on the land and to do what's needed to combat global warming, ozone depletion, water pollution, and other environmental ills.

A New Style for Suburbanites. Living in the suburbs, we're caught between a rock and a hard place. We're stuck between the country and the city, both of which, in their own ways, are more conducive to environmentally gentle living. But we can remake the suburbs, and make them more relevant in this age of disappearing natural resources.

We can work from home, using unbleached recycled paper. We can throw out all the nasty stuff under the sink and replace it with natural cleansers and whiteners. We can use natural fibers and responsibly harvested wood. We can learn how to deal with ants, fleas, and other household pests without chemicals. We can carpool or ride mass transit. We can refuse to join the SUV victory parade. We can plant an organic garden; we can shrink our lawn and fill our landscape with native plants.

Sometimes it's hard to figure out which products we should give up immediately and which we can still use. With so many factors involved, it can be tough to know which changes are most important to our health and which will have the biggest benefits for the environment. So read on to find sound answers and safer alternatives without scolding or guilt tripping. Welcome to the new suburbs.

THE ORGANIC SUBURBANITE AT HOME

PART 1

IN THE KITCHEN

HOW TO

1 The kitchen is the heart and soul of the home, the source of nourishment for family and friends, the place where we tend to gather. Even in the busiest families, someone's always stopping in to grab a quick breakfast or a late-night snack. Do you really need any other reasons to make it more organic?

Analyze Your Appliance Efficiency.

A lot of energy is expended in the kitchen, not necessarily by the chief cook and bottle washer, but by our appliances. Ironically, most of that energy goes to cool things down, and then to heat them up. In fact, more electricity is consumed—and probably wasted—in the kitchen than in any other room of the house. So the best thing you can do in there, environmentally speaking, is to make sure your appliances are operating properly and that you're using them wisely.

If you're buying appliances, always look for the "Energy Star" label. This United States Department of Energy designation is awarded to appliances that exceed minimum government standards for energy conservation. Energy Star labels may be found on clothes washers, refrigerators, dishwashers, and room air conditioners. An appliance receives the Energy Star rating if it is significantly more energy efficient than the minimum government standards, as determined by standard testing procedures. The amount by which an appliance must exceed the government standards is different for each product type rated.

Is Your Refrigerator Running? The fridge is the biggest electricity hog in the house. A typical self-defrosting refrigerator uses more than 1,200 kilowatts of electricity per year. That's more than a clothes dryer and dishwasher combined. It's even more than the amount of electricity used to light a typical house for an entire year. If your refrigerator is more than

Give Your Oven Some Lovin'

Is there a nastier job in the house than cleaning the oven? And there are few household cleansers that are more dangerous than commercial oven cleaners. Not cleaning it might seem like the best option—until something bubbles over and leaves a smoldering puddle on the oven bottom. But you won't need to use a killer chemical oven cleaner if you keep your stove clean with natural cleansers: After every use, wipe the inside of the oven with full-strength 5-percent acidity vinegar after it has cooled down.

Refrigerators today use 42 percent less energy than they did in 1972.

3

15 years old, it's a good time to start shopping for a new Energy Star model to replace it. You'll recover the cost of the new appliance in energy savings within just a few years. Improved insulation and better compressors mean that most late-model Energy Star refrigerators exceed the current minimum energy use standards by at least 20 percent.

Even if you keep your old icebox, make sure it's running at its best. Check the seal to make sure that the cold air is staying inside where it belongs. Place a dollar bill against the jamb while closing the door. If the bill slips to the floor, the seal needs to be replaced.

Check the temperature. Make sure the machine isn't working any harder than it needs to. The most

TIPS

Toxic Fog in the Kitchen

Many conventional dishwasher detergents contain chlorine bleach. The bleach helps to get the dishes clean and sparkling, but the chlorine's potentially harmful vapors escape into the air. When you open the dishwasher to remove the dishes, you're enveloped in a steaming fog of chlorine gas. Breathing the fumes of products with high chlorine content, such as automatic dishwasher detergent, can irritate the lungs. Fortunately, it's easy to rid your kitchen of this toxic fog by choosing a chlorine-free dishwasher detergent.

HOW TO

Tidy Up the Countertop

Ever leave a grocery receipt on the countertop, only to find it after it has gotten soaked and bled ink all over the counter? Here's how to get rid of that nasty stain: Pour 3 or 4 tablespoons of baking soda into a shallow dish. Add enough water to make a paste. Use a toothbrush or other soft-bristled brush to apply the paste to the stain and scrub. If that doesn't completely remove the stain, wipe away the baking soda and soak the stain with lemon juice for 5 minutes. Then reapply the baking soda paste and scrub again.

efficient operation occurs at an interior temperature of 38° to 42°F. Your refrigerator will work most efficiently if you keep the freezer full and if you clean the coils thoroughly every 6 months.

At Home with Your Range. An oven is not a particularly efficient beast, and electric ovens are especially inefficient. If you're buying new and if you have the option, you should always choose gas—either natural or propane—for your range. Both types of gas ranges are about twice as efficient as electric in converting energy to heat for cooking.

Don't overlook the much-maligned microwave as a way of conserving energy. Though it is not the miracle appliance it was once touted to be, microwaving

An automatic dishwasher saves an average of 208 hours of hand labor per year.

is a very efficient way to cook some dishes, especially casseroles. Zapping a dish in a microwave for a few minutes is much more energy-wise than heating an entire oven for 2 hours. By the same token, it's smarter to heat a little toaster oven than a huge range.

Let the Dishwasher Do It. Somewhere along the line, you've probably heard that automatic dishwashers are tremendous water wasters. Most people assume that the most efficient way to wash dishes is the good old-fashioned way, by hand. Neither of these assumptions is true. Hand washing, with the water running, can consume up to 20 gallons of water for a typical sink full of dishes. Using a standard dishwasher, you'll use about 10 to 15 gallons of water per load. But new energy-efficient dishwashers require as few as 5 gallons of water to clean up a load of dirty dishes. And using less water also means less electricity or gas is required to heat the water. Just make sure to run the machine only when you have a full load—*and* when there's no one in the shower.

Life's a Bleach.

Chlorine is ubiquitous in the kitchen. You'll find it as an ingredient in—or as a manufacturing component of—scores of items, from countertop cleansers to dishwasher detergents to bleached coffee filters. (If you don't see the word "chlorine," it may be masquerading on the ingredients list as hypochlorite or sodium hypochlorite.)

Despite its widespread use, there are two problems associated with chlorine bleach. First, its manufacture creates a soup of hazardous and polluting chemicals, including the very toxic dioxin. Second, you may be exposed to dioxins and other chlorine compounds in the product as they leach out. Chlorine was listed as a hazardous air pollutant by the 1990 Clean Air Act, and federal standards govern workers' exposure to chlorine. Exposure to chlorine compounds has been implicated in birth defects, cancer, and developmental disorders.

You can help protect the environment by avoiding bleached paper products whenever possible. Shop for paper towels, napkins, paper plates, and coffee filters that are either unbleached or bleached with safe, nonchlorine products, such as hydrogen peroxide or sodium hydrosulfite.

Good Intentions Down the Drain.

There's nothing like a clogged drain to cause compromises. When the sink is plugged and dishes are piling up, when company is coming or somebody is

(continued on page 10)

HOW TO

Take Out What Nature Didn't Put In

If the produce you buy is not organic, there's a good chance that it contains some pesticide residues. A quick swish under the water faucet won't remove all of them. To make sure you remove the pesticides from the skins of fruits and vegetables, add a few tablespoons of baking soda to a sink full of warm water. Swish the produce in the water and scrub it gently with a soft brush to clean off any unwanted additives.

About two-thirds of all the packaging that's produced is used to wrap up food.

TIPS

What's in Dinner?

A 1995 study by the Environmental Working Group, a nonprofit environmental research organization based in Washington, D.C., reveals some startling facts and figures about the food we eat: A lot of it contains pesticide residue. Much of it has residues from multiple pesticides. And you are what you eat, right?

Of course, the best way to avoid these poisons is to grow your own food. If that's not possible, the next best option is to buy organically grown produce. Even that's not always an option, though, so you should know which foods are most likely to be contaminated by pesticides and which are relatively free of residues. Here they are.

Crop	Samples with Pesticide Residues
Celery	81 percent
Grapes from Chile	79 percent
Cantaloupe from Mexico	76 percent
Nectarines	74 percent
Cherries grown in the United States	71 percent
Peaches	71 percent
Strawberries	70 percent

Here are the fresh fruits and vegetables that had the fewest samples testing positive for pesticides.

Crop	Samples with Pesticide Residues
Avocados	1 percent
Sweet corn	1 percent
Bulb onions	5 percent
Cauliflower	6 percent
Asparagus	14 percent

Some of the scariest findings—all based on U.S. Food and Drug Administration testing—revealed the number of different pesticides found in a single sample of various crops. As many as seven different pesticides were found by the FDA on single samples of apples and peaches grown in the United States. Six pesticides were found on single samples of grapes from Chile, and on lettuce, strawberries, tomatoes, and sweet peppers from the United States and Mexico. At the other end of the scale, only one pesticide was found on one sample among all of the avocado samples that were analyzed. Avoiding pesticides on your produce can sure cut down on your menu options.

Of the 60 billion pounds of plastic produced annually in the United States, less than 3% is recycled.

waiting for the shower, expediency is the rule. We have to get that drain open, come hell or high water. So we reach for the liquid clog remover, let our environmental concerns flow down the drain, and choose not to think about what toxic chemicals we're pouring down the drain—or where they go from there. We'd rather not know where that stuff winds up or what it might do to the septic system, groundwater, or lakes and streams when it reaches them.

Truth is, most drain cleaners contain lye (sodium hydroxide or potassium hydroxide), a very caustic toxin that pollutes water and destroys beneficial bacteria in sewers and sewage treatment plants. When mixed with water, lye is extremely corrosive and will eat through almost anything. That's what makes it such an effective drain opener—it's also what makes it a dangerous poison with no antidote. Using drain cleaners with lye causes breakdowns in the natural sewage decomposition system. Consequently, there's a greater risk of releasing harmful bacteria into the environment. Lye also creates a toxic gas when mixed with chlorine.

Fortunately, though, there are other options you can use to solve your drainage woes, including a few simple preventive measures. For grease buildups, try this natural, safe, and effective approach: Pour ½ cup each of salt and baking soda down the clogged drain. Chase it with 6 cups of boiling water and allow it to work for several hours before flushing the drain with warm water.

Last Resorts. In spite of our best intentions, clogs happen. Here are some safe ways to handle them.

- Slither in. If the sink or toilet is blocked, carefully try to unclog the drain with a plumber's snake.
- Go deep. If the clog is in a sink, take apart the drain catch and remove the obstruction.
- Use water power. Although water from the faucet may not generate enough pressure to clear that clog, water from your garden hose might. Run a garden hose into the sink. Remove any strainers or screens, and force the end of the hose into the drain as far as possible. Wrap rags around the hose at the drain for a decent seal. Have someone turn on the water, full-blast. The force of the water may be enough to clear the clog. Then again, it may not, so make sure your assistant is ready to turn the water off in a hurry.
- Also see page 24 for other nontoxic methods for clearing out clogged drains.

TIPS

Take Out the Compost

The compost bucket on the kitchen counter has become a common sight in gardeners' kitchens, as we divert food wastes from the garbage disposal to the compost bin. Saving food scraps can add a significant amount of material to the compost pile. But it may make us feel bad without realizing it.

A Dutch study showed that folks who keep compostables in the house are three times as likely to be exposed to bacterial toxins and molds that can aggravate asthma and cause coughing and flu-like symptoms. The researchers recommend simply emptying the bucket more frequently.

The average life span of a dishwasher is 9 years.

HOW TO

Keep It Clear

Here's how to keep the drain clean so that drastic (and caustic) measures aren't needed.

- Once a month, pour 1 cup of vinegar down each drain. This natural acid will help prevent buildups of material.
- Use enzyme-based drain cleaners regularly as a preventive measure.
- Make sure all sinks are equipped with drain strainers, and keep them clean.
- Refrain from pouring grease and oil down the drain.

A typical family of four does more than six loads of laundry a week—even more during soccer season. That's more than 240 gallons of dirty water per week down the drain, given that a conventional top-loading washing machine uses an astounding 40 gallons of water per load!

It All Comes Out in the Wash. Over the course of a year, a whole lot of water flows through the average home washing machine and down the drain. The problem is that most of these machines are top-loading, and that's not the most efficient design. The machine's tub has to fill repeatedly to wash, rinse, and wash again. And the clothes take a beating from the agitator. Laundromats, where efficiency is more of a priority, demonstrate a better way: the front-loading washing machine.

Catch Front-Load Fever. Rather than using an agitator, a front-loading washing machine uses a spinning drum to clean clothes. These horizontal-axis or tumble-action machines repeatedly lift and drop clothes, instead of moving them around a central axis. New front-loading machines use 20 to 25 gallons per load, a water savings of 36 percent. So switching to a front-loading machine could save more than 4,000 gallons of water in one year. Less water in the washer means less water to be heated, which translates into even greater energy savings— up to 60 percent over a year's time. As a bonus, clothes are handled more gently, so they last longer.

If a front-loading washing machine seems too radical, there are also more efficient top-loaders on the market. Top-loading Energy Star washers use sensor technology to control the incoming water temperature. To reduce water consumption, they spray clothes with repeated high-pressure rinses to remove soap residues, rather than soaking them in a full tub of rinse water. In the process they use 35 percent less water, save up to 60 percent on energy costs, and require less detergent.

Make Chlorine-Free Bleach

To make hydrogen peroxide bleach, use:

1 part hydrogen peroxide
8 parts water

Mix enough of the ingredients in a dishpan or sink to cover the garment to be bleached. Allow to soak for 5 to 30 minutes. Drain away the bleach solution and rinse the garment in clean water. Be sure to test this bleach solution on a hidden part of your garment before immersing it entirely.

DOING THE LAUNDRY

HOW TO

HOW TO

Try a Gentler Homemade Cleanser

Replace harsh chemical laundry products with these homemade alternatives.

Washing Machine Soap

1 cup of pure soap flakes or powder
2 to 4 tablespoons of washing soda
   (available at large supermarkets)

Add to the washing machine as it is filling with water. Use 2 tablespoons of washing soda for soft water, 4 tablespoons for very hard water.

Delicate Soap for Hand-Washables

¼ cup of soap flakes
1 cup of water
¼ cup of borax

Place ingredients in a saucepan and simmer until mixture reaches uniform consistency. Strain into a glass jar. Cover and store. Mix ¼ cup of soap with hot water to wash a sink full of clothes.

   To cleanse clothes of any remaining soap film, add either ¼ cup of white vinegar or ¼ cup of baking soda to the final rinse.

The average life span of a clothes washer is 13 years.

Your Personal Chlorine Phaseout.

Of all the substances that make up the chemical soup in our environment, none is more pervasive—or more damaging—than chlorine. Thousands of chlorine compounds eat away at the ozone layer, contaminate groundwater, cause cancer and genetic mutations, weaken our immune systems, and do other damage to us and our environment. That's why Greenpeace and other environmental organizations are calling for a planet-wide phaseout of all chlorine products.

Most of the thousands of chlorine products are used in industry—in the manufacture of PVCs, in the bleaching of paper, and in refrigerants. Many, however, also find their ways into our homes. Of course, no one will claim that there's a little hole in the ozone with your name on it because of the chlorine bleach and cleaners you're using, but even those small amounts of home cleansers eventually find their way to the sewage-treatment plant, groundwater, lakes, streams, and air. And a phaseout of these environmental toxins has to start somewhere. So why not in our homes?

You can do your part by refusing to buy or use household products that contain chlorine, such as laundry bleach, laundry and dishwasher detergent, or tub and toilet cleansers. Look for alternative household cleaning products that contain sodium perborate rather than bleach.

Or, you can make your own chlorine-free hydrogen peroxide bleach (see page 12) to remove stains and lighten the color of dreary whites.

Keep in mind, though, that even oxygen bleaches can damage certain kinds of fabrics, so it's always a good idea to test your solutions on a small, discreet spot somewhere on the garment before you submerge the whole thing.

In 1993, the American Public Health Association passed a unanimous resolution urging American

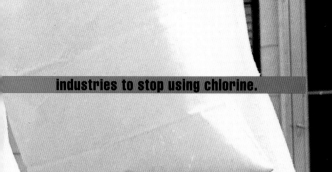

industries to stop using chlorine.

Where Did the Clotheslines Go?

It wasn't too long ago that air-drying clothes was the way everyone did it. Now, virtually all of our clothes go directly from the clothes washer to the clothes dryer. When it comes to dryers, you've got two choices: electric or gas. Gas dryers have a higher sticker price, but because they are much more efficient, they pay for themselves in energy savings in just a few years. In fact, gas dryers require about half as much energy to dry a load of clothes, as do their electric counterparts. So go for gas if you have a choice.

And don't pass up the chance to bypass the clothes dryer altogether whenever a nice day comes along. Using the clothesline won't add a cent to your energy bill, and it gives you a good excuse to spend some time outdoors—instead of in your laundry room—on a sunny day.

HOW TO

Oxygen Bleach for the Washing Machine

Giving up chlorine bleach doesn't mean resigning yourself to stained and dingy clothing. Look for commercial products that contain alternative bleaching compounds. Or, try replacing the chlorine bleach in your laundry routine with a homemade oxygen bleach that you use in your washing machine along with your usual laundry soap or detergent.

Oxygen is an effective bleaching agent. You can put it to work in your laundry room with this solution that incorporates sodium perborate, a natural boron product that you can purchase at pharmacies and hardware stores.

Oxygen Bleach
1½ teaspoons of sodium perborate
¼ cup of water

Mix together and add to the washing machine along with the normal amount of detergent.

As always, it's safest to test your homemade laundry solution on a scrap of fabric or a hidden corner of a garment before using it on an entire load of clothes.

TIPS

Other Chlorine Products to Avoid

Avoiding chlorine is harder than you might suspect—it's lurking in plenty of places outside the laundry room. If your goal is to reduce your household chlorine use, keep an eye on these products, too.

- Bleached paper. Bleaching paper produces more than 1,000 different organochlorine compunds. Many manufacturers now use other chemicals to create chlorine-free paper. Look for those eco-friendly paper products when you shop.
- Polyvinyl chloride (PVC) plastic. Vinyl manufacturing is the largest single user of chlorine. PVC is used to manufacture toys, furniture, window frames, and many, many more products. Burning PVC releases dioxins.
- Cooling units. Refrigerators and air conditioners use chlorine products as cooling agents. Other coolants, including ammonia and hydrocarbons, have recently begun replacing chlorines.
- Bug killers. Pesticides, such as 2,4-D, atrazine, and alachlor are manufactured from chlorines and release chlorine by-products in their manufacture and use.

TIPS

Do Right by Your Dryer

No matter how hard you try to use your clothesline instead of your clothes dryer, there will always be times when the convenience of the dryer wins out over the energy savings of the line. Don't feel bad; you'll return to the clothesline another day. For now, resolve to use your gas or electric clothes dryer as efficiently—and as little—as possible. Here are a few other ways to keep clothes-dryer energy costs under control.

• If you're buying a new dryer, choose a machine with a moisture sensor that shuts off the dryer when the clothes are dry.
• Dry heavy and light clothes separately for maximum efficiency.
• Clean the lint filter after each load.
• Make sure the outside vent is unclogged.
• Use an insulated vent that keeps cold air from leaking into your house when the dryer's not in use.
• Periodically check the tube that runs from your dryer to the outside vent to make sure it's free of blockages that reduce efficiency and create a fire hazard.
• And don't forget to use the clothesline. When weather permits, take the time to hang your clothes outdoors. That little bit of time will pay for itself in energy saved. The clothes will smell better—and last longer, too.

BED AND BATH

About 25 percent of all allergies and 50 percent of all asthmatic diseases can be traced to dust mites.

3 We spend one-third of our lives in our bedroom, but few of us think about how its furnishings affect our health. And it seems as if we spend the rest of our time waiting for the kids to get out of the bathroom. While they're in there, the clock is ticking and the water is running.

A Hotbed of Health Problems. If we have allergies—and millions of Americans do—chances are good that the bedroom is where they start. Most people with allergies are allergic to dust mites. And most dust mites are found in the bedroom. The bed, especially, is a dust-mite breeding ground. To control allergies, keep the mites in check by following these precautions.

- Wash your bedding weekly in hot water, and then dry it in a hot dryer.
- Use a vacuum cleaner equipped with a HEPA (high-efficiency particulate air) filter.
- Use natural organic cotton bedding with a high thread count to reduce dust and lint.
- Cover mattresses, box springs, and pillows in zippered plastic covers.
- Keep windows closed or well screened.
- Vacuum rugs twice a week.

Sleep Tight. Most of us underestimate the importance of our mattresses. Make sure your mattress is composed of natural materials: cotton or wool. Foam mattresses retain heat and don't allow the body to cool properly during the night. That leads to restless sleeping. Foam mattresses may also release formaldehyde and other potentially harmful chemical vapors, which may cause allergies and aggravate chemical sensitivity.

Don't Get Taken to the Cleaners. Watch what you wear, as well as what you sleep under. Opt for natural fabrics and clothes that can be home-laundered. Stay away from the dry cleaners as much as possible. Using a dry cleaner for your clothes, curtains, and bedding contributes to water pollution from runoff of benzene, perchlorethylene, and other carcinogenic and toxic solvents.

The dangers of dry cleaning hit close to home, too: Dry-cleaned fabrics carry traces of carcinogenic solvents and allergens and continue to release fumes from those solvents as they hang in your closet or at your windows. Perchlorethylene, for example, comes home on those fabrics and can vaporize in your house. Exposure to this chemical can increase your risk of liver cancer. If you do have something dry-cleaned, hang it in a well-ventilated area or outdoors, if weather permits. Ideally, it's better to avoid dry cleaning altogether and buy clothing and window coverings made of fabrics that you can launder at home.

The Clothes Make the Environmentalist. Folks love cotton. It feels great, it looks good, and it's easy to care for. We love the idea of wearing a natural fabric, too. But growing cotton is one of the most chemically intensive forms of farming. Of all the pesticides used worldwide, one-quarter of them are applied to cotton fields. And at least five of the major pesticides used on cotton in the United States (cyanazine, dicofol, naled, propargite, and trifluralin) are known cancer-causing chemicals.

Before that cotton can become clothing, it's also treated with silicone, heavy metals, ammonia, formaldehyde, chemical dyes, and more. But organic cotton is minimally processed and may not even require dyeing. Now *that's* natural.

TIPS

Cleaner, Greener Dry Cleaning

Environmentalism has gradually infiltrated the dry-cleaning industry, and there are now eco-friendly cleaners cropping up across the country. Some use a nontoxic, safe hydrocarbon dry-cleaning solvent in place of the toxic and ozone-depleting perchlorethylene ("perc") used by most dry cleaners. Others use Exxon DF-2000 synthetic petroleum solvent, which can be used in much smaller quantities than perc. One gallon of the stuff will clean as much as 1,000 pounds of clothing.

Showers account for nearly one-third of all household water use.

TIPS

Wet Is Better Yet

Even the safest and most efficient cleaning solvents are still solvents—chemical compounds that have the potential to harm our health and the health of the environment. If you're really interested in avoiding the risks associated with exposure to cleaning compounds, take a look at "wet cleaning."

Confronted by the health and environmental costs of dry cleaning (it's not healthy for the people who work in those places either), some dry cleaners are converting their shops to a water-based cleaning process. By using technologically advanced washing equipment and other innovations, these businesses strive to provide comparable clothes-cleaning quality without the hazards of dry cleaning.

Green and Clean in the Bathroom. These

days, it seems that every supermarket features an entire aisle that's dedicated to bathroom cleansers: foams for the tub, sprays for the sink, and little tablets for the toilet. But check the labels. These cleansers and cleaning supplies contain all manner of nasty ingredients, from chlorine bleach to fungicides to bactericides. You don't really need all that stuff just to clean the tub—or even to remove those dreaded "tough stains."

If you do check the ingredients list on those cleansers, often you'll find that beyond all the tongue-twisting chemical names, many cleansers contain very simple ingredients, including two great natural cleansers: vinegar and baking soda. Chances are, you already have them in your cupboard, even if you've never given them a thought on cleaning day.

Vinegar should be in every cleaning cabinet. Vinegar's natural acidity allows it to remove stains, cut through grease, and kill mold and mildew. It also eliminates odors. Fill a spray bottle with undiluted 5 percent white vinegar and keep it in the bathroom. You'll get plenty of use out of it.

Baking Soda: True Grit in a Box. Most of us already know that baking soda is a great deodorant. Just place an opened box in the refrigerator, closet, or cupboard to absorb nasty smells. But it's also a great cleanser because of its natural—though safe—grittiness.

Refresh a Moldy Shower Curtain

Use undiluted vinegar and a sponge to scrub light mold and mildew from shower curtains. If the curtain has gotten downright disgusting with mildew, use vinegar in the washing machine. Simply toss the curtain and two or three towels (to aid in scrubbing) in the washing machine. Set the cycle to hot and add detergent and 1 cup of vinegar. Run the machine on its normal cycle, and the shower curtain will emerge sparkling.

Use the Faucet

That's what it's there for. Don't let the water run when you brush your teeth, wash your face or hands, or shave. This can save 3 to 7 gallons of water per minute.

- Baking soda will take care of even the toughest mildew stains in the tub. Just mix 2 cups of baking soda with ½ cup of warm water to make a paste. Use a toothbrush or other soft-bristled brush to scrub away mildew. Rinse with warm water.
- To clean stains from marble, sinks, or wooden counters, make a paste by mixing 1 cup of baking soda with ¼ cup of water. Rub the paste on the stain, then rinse with warm water. You can use the same paste to "remove" (actually, fill) scratches and cuts from laminated countertops. Apply the paste in a circular motion and watch scratches disappear.
- Combine the powers of baking soda and vinegar to clear a hair-clogged drain: Pour 1 cup of baking soda down the drain, then chase it with 1 cup of vinegar. After 10 minutes, flush the drain with hot water.
- Also see page 10 for other methods of unclogging troublesome drains.

Make Windows and Mirrors Sparkle. Mix equal parts vinegar and water. Add 1 tablespoon of rubbing alcohol per quart to aid in drying. Spray to clean windows or mirrors. Use crumpled newspaper or coffee filters to wipe clean, as they contain no lint.

Straight Flush in the Bathroom. It's no wonder that Brits call the bathroom a water closet. A lot of H_2O flows in and out of that small room every day, what with baths, showers, shaving, and flushes. In fact, up to half the water consumed in a home is used in the bathroom. And in most cases, that's twice as much as necessary. You can save a lot of water with some simple retrofits, and you'll hardly notice the difference.

Change Your Showerhead. Chances are your showerhead uses about 5 gallons of water per minute. Multiply that by your leisurely 15-minute shower, and that's a lot of water down the drain. However, you can still enjoy that shower—and save half the water—by installing a new, efficient showerhead. Old showerheads use up to 6 gallons of water per minute (gpm) but, as of January 1994, all new showerheads were required to have a flow of 2½ gpm or less.

You can cut your water use even more dramatically: Install a switch shower head that lets you shut off the water flow at the showerhead while you're soaping. Take a Navy shower: Get wet, turn off the water, soap and scrub, then briefly turn the water back on to rinse.

An average family can save roughly 17,000 gallons of water per year by installing efficient showerheads and faucet aerators. Faucet aerators add air to the spray to lower the flow. Most aerators reduce the water flow significantly—from 2 to 4 gallons per minute, to less than 1 gallon per minute.

Rethink Your Throne. The biggest water savings can come from the john, the throne, the toilet. About one-third of all the water used in the house gets flushed away. In most cases, that's way more water than is needed. Old toilet models had big tanks full of water and used up to 5 gallons per flush. Newer models are much more water efficient, getting by with a maximum of 1.6 gallons per flush (gpf). You might think that these water-conserving toilets don't flush well, but some models use pressure from the household's water supply to generate a more forceful flush. These pressure-assisted toilets may be noisy and more expensive than gravity-flush models, but they do a better job of staying clean and odor-free while conserving water with every flush.

Many municipalities offer rebates on low-flow toilet purchases and free removal of old toilets. If no such program is available where you live, you can easily retrofit your old toilet to make it more water efficient. Place a plastic quart bottle filled with water in the toilet tank, taking care that it doesn't interfere with the flushing mechanism. Or buy a specially designed "displacement bag" to hang inside the tank. Most families flush eight times a day. That's 8 gallons a day, or nearly 3,000 gallons per year, of water saved.

Polish That Throne and Tidy the Tub

Forget about the toxic concoctions that are sold to put a shine on tub, tile, and toilet. Instead of sloshing cleansers containing chlorine, or even hydrochloric acid, around in your bathroom, consider the merits of vinegar. It costs less, it's safe enough to eat, and it works.

You don't need all that chemical stuff to keep the toilet bowl clean. You can use white vinegar to remove stains.

Pour 1 cup of vinegar into the toilet. Let it soak, then brush and flush. If stains remain, flush, sprinkle baking soda on stains, and brush and flush again.

Use undiluted 5-percent vinegar to clean that ugly grime between shower tiles and around tub and sink fixtures. Soak a toothbrush in full-strength vinegar and use it to scrub the grout between tiles. It's equally useful for scrubbing around fixtures. Use a sponge or cloth to wipe down shower stalls with full-strength vinegar to clean water spots and soap scum. Let the vinegar soak in for a few minutes, then rinse with clear water.

4

As a working person, the best thing you can do for the environment is leave your car in the driveway and stay put. The suburbs were built as bedroom communities where workers get in their cars each morning and drive away. But the suburbs turn out to be a good place for a home office, too.

Give Telecommuting a Try. These days more and more people are telecommuting or working in home-based offices—even in the suburbs. And that's good for the environment.

In large part, we can thank the computer for making it possible. But that doesn't mean we have to go out and upgrade to the newest screaming fast machine every six months.

Computers, in home operation, are environmentally benign. Their energy use is negligible. On average, computers account for the use of 18 kilowatt hours (kwh) of electricity per year per household. Compare that to a washing machine at 99 kwh, a TV at 360 kwh, or a refrigerator at more than 1,000 kwh. That's why it's no big deal to leave a computer running all day. In fact, leaving it on is preferable to shutting it off and turning it on several times a day. That causes wear and tear that can burn up the machine.

Keep Your Computer Green. Running a computer may be benign, but the same can't be said for computer manufacturing. Making new computers requires a lot of plastic, a lot of metal, and—worst of all—a lot of solvents to make those speedy new chips. The single largest source of water pollution in the state of Vermont is the computer industry because of the solvents used in chip manufacture that are being washed into the groundwater.

So, to be green, keep that computer running as long as you can. Upgrade as necessary by adding a larger hard drive or more memory. When it's finally time to buy a newer model, don't just toss the old one—donate the machine to a nonprofit agency, or give it to Grandma so she can send e-mails to the entire family. When shopping for a new computer, look for an Energy Star–labeled model to get the most energy-efficient machine.

Cut Paper Use, Not Trees. As long as it's in running condition, you can use your computer to reduce all kinds of waste.

• Work on-screen rather than on paper (that you'll discard later) whenever possible.

Commuting to and from work accounts for one-third of all private auto mileage.

THE GREEN
OFFICE

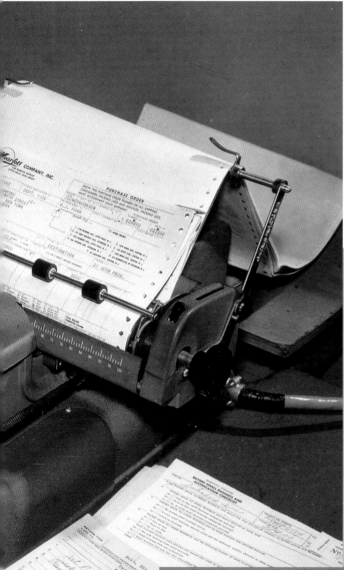

- Send faxes via your computer modem, rather than printing and sending them conventionally.
- Use e-mail rather than snail mail whenever possible.
- Use Web sites, chat rooms, or networks for real-time conferencing rather than physically gathering people from distant locations.

Don't Be a Dim Bulb about Lighting. If you work at home, chances are you will burn a lot more energy just to illuminate your workspace. In the average home, fully one-quarter of electric energy used in the house goes toward providing light.

Apart from getting in the habit of turning off lights when you leave a room, there are some easy and inexpensive ways to cut light use significantly.

Getting the Lead Out

The Commonwealth of Massachusetts has banned the disposal of computer monitors and television sets in its landfills and incinerators. Why? Lead. The average cathode ray tube, the heart of the monitor, contains 8 to 10 pounds of lead. If a tube is dumped in a landfill, lead can, over time, seep into the groundwater—another darn good reason to keep using your computer as long as possible.

Americans make 400 billion photocopies per year.

THE GREEN OFFICE

First, get rid of those halogen torchière lamps. In addition to being fire hazards, they are electricity hogs that require 10 times as much power to provide an amount of light equivalent to an incandescent bulb. Even better than incandescent are compact fluorescent bulbs. Although they cost more than incandescent bulbs, the compact fluorescents burn longer and require much less energy, so you'll easily recover the difference in price over the long run.

TIPS

Avoiding That Unhealthy Glow

Computer monitors give off low levels of a regular vegetable soup of radiation, from x-rays to ultraviolet, microwave, and radiowave radiation, as well as static electricity and something called "pulsating fields of energy" that may or may not cause the skin to become "excited and overheated." Most studies of these types of radiation indicate that there is little cause for computer users to be concerned about exposure to such forces. But we are talking about radiation, and there are options if you're worried about what such exposure might do to you (or to your baby, if you're pregnant). If you want to be extra-safe, consider equipping your computer with an LCD (liquid-crystal display) monitor, which emits less radiation than a regular monitor (but costs significantly more).

TIPS

Eco-Friendly Office Supplies

Here are a few other ways to watch out for the environment—and your health—when you're working at home.

Printer. Have your printer's cartridge refilled rather than buying an entirely new toner cartridge. Even small inkjet cartridges can be refilled with a do-it-yourself inkjet toner refiller.

Paper. Buy recycled and unbleached paper whenever possible. Reuse paper for scrap, for taking telephone messages, or for the kids' artwork. Buy a shredder—you can even get a hand-powered model—and shred used printer paper rather than tossing it in the trash. Use the shreddings to pad packages for shipping, mulch your garden with them, or toss them into your compost pile.

Other office stuff. Solvents from correction fluid, highlighters, and permanent markers all are harmful to the environment, and routinely inhaling their fumes may cause health problems. Make sure your home office is adequately ventilated, and use natural and safe alternatives whenever possible. Look for the Art & Craft Materials Institute "Nontoxic" or "Health" labels, which certify that certain office supplies, as well as children's art supplies, are safe and nontoxic.

One-fifth of all wood harvested in the world ends up in paper.

ORGANIC FOR
YOUR OFFSPRING

The suburbs are so kid-friendly: miles of curving streets for biking, acres of green grass to roll in. Only recently have we started to realize some of suburbia's hidden costs to our children, like the methods used to get all that grass so lush, green, and dandelion-free.

Per Pound: The Perils of Pesticides.

We'd do anything for our kids. We make sure they don't eat too much sugar or watch too much TV. We conscientiously strap them into their car seats, then we worry about accidents and injuries. But most parents overlook one serious health threat—pesticides—in the house, in the yard, and on their food.

In 1993, the National Academy of Sciences released a 5-year study, "Pesticides in the Diets of Infants and Children," confirming that infants and children are generally more susceptible to pesticides than adults, and concluding that current regulations do not adequately protect children from pesticides. The study said that there's a strong chance that ingesting multiple pesticides from foods may cause acute organophosphate poisoning in kids.

That's a good reason to grow your own food because many supermarket foods are tainted with pesticides (see page 8). Buying organic produce is another way to protect your family. And when organically grown produce isn't available, it helps to know which supermarket foods typically carry the most—or the least—pesticide residues.

Make Your House a No-Spray Zone. Never mind the bugs, it's kids who may be paying the price for pesticide use in and around the house. Recent research suggests a link between pesticide use in a home and the incidence of childhood cancer. According to a University of North Carolina study, using pest strips in the home elevated children's risk of leukemia, brain tumor, and lymphoma. The use of pesticides in the yard was associated with a four-fold increase in the risk of soft tissue sarcoma. (In another study performed at Stanford University School of Medicine, researchers found that people who developed Parkinson's disease later in life were more than twice as likely to have used pesticides in and around the home than those who didn't develop Parkinson's.)

For the sake of your kids' health (and your own), make your home a pesticide-free zone. Do not use bug killers in the house, especially not in the kitchen or in a child's room. And don't call in exterminators

In 1999, doctors prescribed lindane more than 2 million times to treat head lice and scabies.

to handle insect problems—there are worse things than a few ants in the pantry.

Safe Swinging. Cuts, scrapes, and bruises are all par for the course when kids play. All the more reason to make sure their play gyms are not made of materials that contain—and may release—dangerous chemicals. Do not use pressure-treated lumber or used railroad ties to build playground equipment. Instead, use naturally weather-resistant lumber such as redwood and cedar, or composites made from wood and recycled plastic.

HOW TO

Give Them a Happy Landing

Make sure kids have a happy landing by providing a layer of safe cushioning material under swings. A thin layer of mulch may look OK, but follow the depths listed below to create a genuinely safe place to land when kids fall—or jump—from the swing.

Sand: 12 inches
Pea gravel: 6 inches
Rice hulls: 6 inches
Wood chips: 6 inches

If you use wood chips or rice hulls under a play structure, turn them regularly to promote drying so they don't become moldy.

HOW TO

Don't Let the Head Bugs Bite

It's mortifying when you get the call from the school saying your child is being sent home because he or she has head lice. And you'll do just about anything to get rid of those creepy little bugs and get the kid back to school. That might mean using a shampoo that contains lindane, a highly toxic pesticide and a suspected carcinogen. But there's no need to take that chance. With patience, you can bring a head lice infestation under control using an oil-based shampoo and a special comb designed to remove lice and their eggs (called nits).

• Make sure your kids tell you as soon as a head lice infestation is noted at school. Immediately begin checking them for lice, using a flashlight and a comb.

• Even if you find none, begin shampooing with a coconut oil, olive oil, or tea tree oil shampoo and the warmest water your child can comfortably withstand. (Children's scalps are very sensitive to heat, so start with lukewarm water and increase the temperature gradually.)

• If you find lice, eggs, or nits, comb them out using a special comb designed for that purpose (the combs are available in pharmacies). First, coat the hair with vegetable oil, then begin combing out one section at a time, dipping the comb into a bowl of hot, slightly soapy water after each pass to remove any trapped nits. Wash the hair twice after you've finished combing.

• Wash hats and bedding in hot water and dry in a hot dryer.

• For severe infestations, shampoo with a pyrethrum head lice shampoo. Pyrethrum is an insecticide derived from chrysanthemums. It's a safer choice than lindane; however, it is still a very potent insecticide. Some children do have minor reactions, such as rashes and itching, to pyrethrin-based shampoos.

TIPS

Safe at Home?

We tend to relax when our kids are at home, thinking that here, of all places, they are safe. But hazards come in many shapes (and bright colors), and even the most popular and widely available toys and playthings may contain harmful substances.

- Swing sets and playground equipment are often made from pressure-treated lumber that can leach arsenic.
- Soft, chewable toys made from PVC plastic may release organochlorides and dioxin.
- Paints, adhesives, and markers may contain hazardous solvents.

Even at home, keeping your kids safe means making careful choices. Avoid play sets built from treated wood; don't go hog-wild buying brightly colored plastic toys, and keep the play area well-ventilated. Use water-based, nontoxic markers and paints for art projects. And always read the label on art supplies you give to your children, and be wary of products that don't carry information about their ingredients as well as evidence of certification from the Art & Craft Materials Institute.

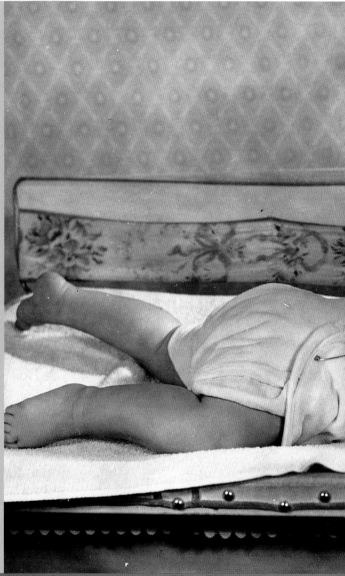

About 1,300 tons of the cadmium in the waste stream—50 to 75 percent—

comes from discarded batteries.

Diaper Wars: Cloth vs. Disposable.

A lot of trees have laid down their lives to produce enough paper to print all of the warring studies about which is more harmful to the environment: cloth or disposable diapers. There have been several conflicting cradle-to-grave studies that consider the environmental impact of the manufacture, maintenance, and disposal of both types of diapers. Manufacture of disposable diapers, of course, consumes a lot of paper and plastic: some 1,265,000 metric tons of wood pulp and 75,000 metric tons of plastic every year. And, since we dispose of 18 billion of them per year, those diapers contribute to the ongoing pressure on our rapidly filling landfills. Cloth diapers, on the other hand, are made from a naturally renewable source: cotton. But growing that cotton requires water and pesticides, and causes erosion. But the chief environmental impact from cloth diapers comes from the laundering they require: All of the water and all of the energy needed to heat the water.

The conflicting arguments can make you dizzy. So what's a parent to do? Here's a simple rule of thumb: Whenever you have a choice of any product, choose reusable over disposable. Choose natural material made from renewable sources over petroleum-based products. That makes the decision easy. It's cloth. Any time you throw out 18 billion of anything, it's a waste disposal problem. And laundering cloth diapers yourself will use less water and energy than sending them to a diaper service.

Need just a little more incentive? Some child-rearing experts believe that children who wear cloth diapers learn to use the toilet earlier than kids in disposables. The high absorbency of disposables makes a wet diaper more comfortable than a soggy cloth one.

Supermarkets are set up to seduce us into buying more than we need from aisles filled with unnecessary "necessities." A lot of environmental waste and pollution starts here. But smart choices at the supermarket can make big differences in the landfill, in air quality, and in our health.

Shop Local, Think Global.
So many of the choices we make in the supermarket are based on benefits to our health. But our choices affect the health of the environment, too, even if that information isn't spelled out in a government-mandated label that's slapped on every item.

Local Produce. Buy local. A tremendous amount of energy is wasted just bringing that out-of-season tomato or foreign cantaloupe to your market. The more we buy crops out of season—strawberries in March in Vermont or sweet corn in December in Minnesota—the higher the energy cost rises. Buying locally means eating seasonally, and enjoying local crops while they're at their peak of freshness.

Buy fruits, vegetables, and grains. Among the many reasons people have for becoming vegetarians, one is environmental. Producing vegetables has a much lighter impact on the earth than does producing meat. Fully three-quarters of the water used in the United States goes to support agriculture. And three-quarters of that goes to raising livestock and poultry for meat. Raising vegetables, fruits, and grains is much more efficient than raising meat, in terms of the water used in the process.

Organic Produce. While you're shopping for produce, buy organic for two reasons: To protect yourself and your family from possible serious heath effects, and to support an industry that farms the land responsibly. The Food and Drug Administration (FDA) and the Environmental Protection Agency (EPA) have found that a significant amount of our supermarket produce tests positive for pesticide residue. According to research from the Environmental Working Group, the worst offenders are celery, Chilean grapes, cantaloupe, nectarines, cherries and peaches, and strawberries. Among the safest commodities are avocados, sweet corn, bulb onions, and cauliflower. You can avoid all of those pesticides simply by paying more for the security of certified organic produce. And if the supermarket you shop in doesn't carry organic produce—or carries only a small or substandard selection—speak to the produce manager and make it clear that you're willing to spend your money on locally grown organic fruits and vegetables.

The number of different pesticides found by the FDA on food samples in 1993: 91.

SMART
SUPERMARKET
SHOPPING

Look for the certified organic label, which now means the product meets stringent federal guidelines. Choose organic products over products labeled IPM, or integrated pest management, a catch-all designation that means a crop was monitored to more accurately time chemical applications. IPM does not mean the product was raised without chemicals.

Aerosols. This is one aisle where consumer mobilization caused change. After the word got out about the damage caused to the ozone layer by the aerosol propellants CFCs (chlorofluorocarbons), they were banned from aerosol cans 15 years ago. Aerosol sprays now contain the less-harmful (but still ozone-depleting) HCFCs (hydrochlorofluorocarbons). If you're sincerely interested in the integrity of the ozone layer—and its ability to protect us from harmful solar radiation—it's best to stay away from aerosols completely.

Detergents. Avoid detergents and other laundry additives that contain chlorine bleach. Instead, buy products with oxygen bleach (sodium perborate), also sold as color-safe bleach. See "Your Personal Chlorine Phaseout" on page 15 for instructions on making your own chlorine-free laundry products.

Cleansers. Avoid kitchen and bathroom cleansers that contain bleach. Don't buy disinfectants, as they contain mildew-killing pesticides and are unnecessary. Antibacterial soaps and cleansers also are unnecessary, and may promote the development of resistant strains of bacteria.

Paper Products. Buy unbleached paper (especially coffee filters) whenever possible. Look for paper towels, napkins, and lunch bags made from recycled material. Make sure they have been recycled from post-consumer waste without the use of chlorine.

TIPS

Check Your Gallons per Serving

Growing and processing the food we eat takes water—to moisten the soil for crops and to quench the cattle's thirst, as well as to wash the produce before it reaches the supermarket.

Here's how various foods stack up in terms of the gallons of water needed to produce a serving, according to the Los Angeles Department of Water and Power.

Food	Gallons of water per serving
Tomatoes	3
French fries	6
Lettuce	6
Sugar	8
Wheat bread	15
Apples	16
Oranges	22
Cantaloupe	51
Milk	65
Watermelon	100
Eggs	136
Chicken	408
Hamburger	1,303
Steak	2,607

Plastic Bags and Wraps. You may be able to find garbage bags, food-storage and sandwich bags, wraps, and films, shop for brands that contain natural cellulose fibers. They're made from renewable resources, such as corn, rather than from petroleum.

But even these more environmentally responsible products will eventually wind up in a landfill. Whenever possible, reuse food storage containers and replace plastic wrap with waxed paper.

Recycling Reality

Most of us assume that if we toss our collection of plastic bags into the supermarket recycling bin, we've done our duty. Our conscience is clean. But hold on. It's not that simple. Have you removed every "contaminant" from those bags? You had better. If that bunch of bags contains plastic snack packages, food wrap, dark-colored bags, or bags with drawstrings or plastic handles—or even sales receipts, coupons, staples, or coins—it will be rejected at the recycling facility and tossed in the trash. In effect, it will have taken a long ride for nothing. Paper bags have much more potential for recovery. In fact, one-third of all paper and paperboard packaging is being recovered in America. That compares to only 12 percent of other packaging material.

Containers. Most of us have calmed our conscience pangs about buying products in plastic containers, reasoning that we'll recycle them anyway. Not so fast. Only a small percentage of plastics are recyclable and, of those recyclable plastics, only about 1 percent actually get recycled.

How can you tell the good plastic from the bad plastic? Check the bottom of the container for its classification. Of the seven classifications, only two currently have a real potential for being recycled: #1 PET (polyethylene terephthalate) and #2 HDPE (high density polyethylene). Anything else goes straight to the landfill. But check with your municipal recycling agency to find out what's accepted there and what's not.

Bear in mind that only a small percentage of this "recyclable" plastic actually gets recycled into other products, and even those will someday find their way into a landfill. Whenever you have the option, buy products that are packaged in glass or aluminum. They're definitely recyclable.

Finally, when you get to the checkout, perhaps slightly exhausted by the many choices you've already made, you'll be asked to make one more important decision: plastic or paper.

That Is the Question.
Paper or plastic? It's a question that symbolizes the dilemma of the modern suburban environmentalist. We want to do the right thing and live lightly on the earth. Yet there are so many factors involved, it's often hard to sort out the environmentally correct answer. In the end, we often just shrug and avoid the question altogether. However, there is a clear answer to this question, and here it is—once and for all.

Each American uses about 190 pounds of plastic per year. Nearly one-third of that is packaging.

Most of us assume that "paper" is the correct answer to the grocery-store question. Paper bags seem inherently more environmentally friendly than plastic ones. In fact, it's true that paper is made from a renewable resource (trees), that it is recyclable, and that it decomposes relatively rapidly.

However, paper is not entirely benign. The problem with paper comes at the front end, when it's manufactured.

Paper? Most supermarket bags are made from virgin paper, containing zero recycled content. The manufacturing process causes a whole host of problems.

- It requires the use of toxic herbicides and pesticides in our forests.
- It damages soil and consumes trees.
- It releases dioxins into the air and PCBs (polychlorinated biphenyls) into the water.

Or Plastic? Plastic, on the other hand, is not so easily recycled. Of course, it can't be composted at home, and many communities do not accept plastic grocery bags in their recycling programs. Plastic supermarket bags also contain no recycled content.

- They are made from petroleum, which is a nonrenewable resource.
- Their production and processing require the use of many toxic chemicals. In 1986, the Environmental Protection Agency ranked the 20 chemicals whose production generates the most hazardous waste. Five of the top six—propylene, phenol, ethylene, polystyrene, and benzene—were chemicals commonly used by the plastic industry.
- They will not naturally decompose in a landfill, although plastic bags in landfills take up 70 percent to 80 percent less space than paper bags.
- They contaminate the oceans.

And the Winner Is . . . If you add it all up, the manufacture and disposal of a single paper bag creates more pollution than the manufacture of a single plastic bag. But "paper or plastic?" is a trick question. The real answer is "neither." The best solution is to carry a reusable cloth or net bag. But that's not always practical. If you find yourself in the store without one, here's how to minimize the environmental impact of whichever bag you choose.

It's what you do with the bag that matters most. You can cut your bag use (and their impact on the environment) in half while you're in the checkout line. Don't let the bagger use two or even three bags when one will do. Tell them to "Pack 'em full." Then, when you get home, reuse the bags.

• Bring paper bags back to the store to use again the next time you shop. Some stores will give you a few cents credit for each paper bag you reuse.

• Fill paper bags with grass clippings and toss them in the compost heap.

• Cut paper bags flat and lay them in the garden as mulch, then cover with grass clippings or bark chips.

• Return plastic bags to the store for recycling.

• Use plastic bags to line the trash can instead of buying virgin plastic garbage bags.

TIPS

Billions of Bags

Tons of paper bags produced in United States in 1995	1,990,000
Tons of paper bags recycled	340,000 (17.1%)
Tons of plastic bags produced in United States in 1995	2,890,000
Tons of plastic bags recycled	80,000 (2.8%)

CONTROLLING
HOUSEHOLD
PESTS

Few of us are willing to put up with creepy-crawlies in the house. The occasional moth or even a hidden spider, sure. But greater numbers of multilegged visitors tend to make us cast aside our organic intentions in a hurry. Before you grab the bug-death-in-a-can, consider some safer solutions.

The Ants Come Marching. Someone has figured that there are more than one quadrillion ants on the earth. Sometimes it seems as though they're all congregating in your kitchen. Like baseball and barbecues, ants are a sure sign of summer in the suburbs. One day there's nary a one to be seen, but the next day they're swarming all over your counters, cupboards, and floors. But wait! There's no need to blast them (and your kitchen) with a toxic spray. There are other safer, more effective ways to control these little pests.

However unwelcome they are, compared to other household pests, ants are relatively benign. They don't carry diseases or pathogens; very few of the indoor ants bite and, in fact, they may do us a favor by preying on more harmful insects.

Still, no one wants ants swarming through the house. No one wants to eat food that ants have crawled over. But you don't have to put up with that if you know what ants like and you are diligent about thwarting them.

Track 'Em. First, figure out where the ants are coming from. Ants start outdoors, and most become a problem only when they find their way indoors. Your mission is to seek out and block their entryways. Find the ant trail and track the army of ants back to their entry point to the house: a hole, crack, or whatever. Seal it up with caulk.

Soap 'Em. Once the ants have led you to their entry, you can get to work on wiping them out. Spray any ants you find with soapy water, or wipe them away with a sponge dipped in soapy water. The soapy spray will kill the ants, and it also erases the pheromone markers that guide other ants along the trail into your house.

Lock Up the Food. Limiting access to your food is the most important thing you can do to prevent all sorts of indoor pest problems. If ants show up, they're there for a reason, and that reason almost always is food. Some are attracted to sweets, others to fats and greases. Whatever they're after, your job is to make sure they can't get to it. Pack your food in ant-proof

Insects make up 60 percent of the 1.75 million species of animals on the earth.

TIPS

containers such as glass jars, canisters with tight lids, or sealed plastic containers.

Make a Moat. If there's food—or trash—that can't be stored away, you can make ant moats of water mixed with a little detergent. Ants can cross plain water, but adding detergent breaks the surface tension so the ants can't float across.

Keep the Kitchen Clean. Make sure there aren't any other food sources to invite ants into your kitchen.
- Wipe counters frequently with soapy water.
- Rinse cans and bottles before throwing them out or putting them in the recycling bin.
- Sweep the floor frequently.
- Clean the pet dishes regularly and don't leave pet food sitting out after Fido finishes a meal.

If that doesn't do it, and ants continue to be a problem, set out natural baits that contain boric acid. Place them along ant trails according to instructions on the package.

The Cockroach, King of Pests.

Cockroaches make the skin crawl. There's something creepy and menacing about them. Maybe it's the way they scurry across the floor or—ugh!—the counter when you turn on the light. There's something disheartening and frustrating about them, the way they seem indestructible. There's something embarrassing about them, the way they imply that the house is dirty. Even the way they crunch when you step on them is repulsive.

Safe, Natural Pest Control

Exterminators don't use it and most homeowners know little about it, but boric acid is a miracle pest killer. A sure-fire stomach poison to many insects, it is safe enough for humans to use as an eyewash and an ingredient in contact lens solution. (However, in its pure form, boric acid is toxic if ingested, can irritate mucous membranes and the respiratory system if inhaled, and can cause burns when it makes skin contact. So, don't use it near children or pets.)

When ingested by insects, boric acid disrupts the action of bacteria in their stomachs and causes the critters to starve to death. However, boric acid is not a quick fix. It may take 5 to 10 days to kill ants or roaches. But a single application, if kept dry, will last for years. Boric acid is available as a dust or in tablets for baits.

There is another class of extremely safe pesticides called sorptive dusts. These products kill insects by absorbing and/or abrading the protective waxy outer layer of their bodies, causing them to dehydrate, and then die.

One very useful organic dust in this category is diatomaceous earth (DE), a mined product made up of the fossilized remains of tiny single-celled creatures known as diatoms. It is both abrasive and absorptive to insect bodies. DE is virtually harmless to mammals, although it's best to wear a dust mask or respirator when applying it.

Don't confuse pool-grade diatomaceous earth with the type sold for organic pest control; the DE used in swimming pools is chemically treated and is a respiratory hazard.

The adult life of an American cockroach lasts about 1½ years.

Cockroaches, however, are not serious health threats. In fact, the Centers for Disease Control (CDC) have removed them from their list of public-health pests. But cockroaches do contaminate food with feces and other organic waste. And cockroaches are believed to be a widespread source of allergens that contribute to and aggravate asthma, especially in inner cities. No one wants them around.

Every year Americans spend a billion dollars spraying to control cockroaches. Some of the most toxic chemicals known to man have been unleashed against them. Guess what? They're still here. And they'll probably be around at least as long as we are. But you don't need fumigators and gas masks to battle cockroaches. You can control them with safe materials and good sanitary practices.

Clean Up Your Act. Make top-notch sanitation your first line of defense. If cockroaches are a problem in your building, lock up that food, even if it's a pack of gum on the counter. Scrub the counters and floors. Clean that stuff out from the cracks between the counters and the refrigerator or stove.

Trap 'Em. Use nontoxic sticky traps to capture cockroaches. Don't scrimp on the number of traps. Use as many as eight in a typical kitchen. Put them along the perimeters of rooms where roaches roam. Don't expect the cockroaches to go out of their way to get themselves trapped.

Seal Cracks. Hunt for cracks that may provide entry near walls and windows; seal them with caulk.

Dust 'Em. Apply boric acid in cracks and crevices where cockroaches congregate. One application should be sufficient because boric acid remains active indefinitely, as long as it's kept dry. (Don't use boric acid where it could pose a hazard to children or pets.)

Natural Flea Fighting.

When the pet starts scratching, and you spot a flea or two hopping on the carpet, and you start feeling itchy all over, even the most dedicated organic householder may feel inclined to throw caution and common sense to the wind in an effort to eradicate those little pests. Hang a poison-impregnated collar around your cat's neck? No problem. Dip the dog into a tub of carcinogens? Sure. How about spraying a nerve poison all over the house? Whatever it takes.

Fortunately, it doesn't require such drastic measures to stop a flea infestation. There are plenty of natural and effective remedies, as well as safe, sensible preventive measures.

Comb. The best way to control fleas is to find them before they get out of hand. Use a flea comb to check your pets regularly. Its finely spaced teeth will do a good job of removing fleas and their eggs from your pet's coat.

Vacuum and Wash. Regular and thorough vacuuming will eliminate flea eggs (be sure to change the vacuum bag frequently). Vacuum all carpets twice a week during flea season. Wash pet bedding monthly in hot water; more often if the infestation is severe.

Borax. Borax (sodium teraborate) is a slow-acting flea cure that's best used to clear up light infestations. Just sprinkle it on carpets, and the crystals dissolve the waxy protective coating on fleas, eggs, and larvae. Because its killing action is mechanical, not chemical, fleas cannot build up resistance to borax. Allow 2 to 3 weeks for all fleas to disappear.

Hormones. One of the best flea preventives, natural or not, is methoprene, sold as Precor. This synthetic insect growth regulator is completely nontoxic to all other forms of life, but it prevents the fleas from

53

reproducing. It won't kill the fleas that are already there, but it effectively sterilizes them so they don't continue to populate your home. Spray according to label directions to cover carpets, furniture, and floors. One treatment lasts up to 7 months.

Natural Food Supplements. There are several food additives that are touted as flea repellents. In theory these supplements, usually containing brewer's yeast, garlic, and sulfur, make a pet less attractive to fleas. Their efficacy is a matter of some debate.

Herbal Spray. A relatively new class of natural flea spray contains oil of erigeron (also known as flea-bane), which reputedly dissolves the protective coating of flea bodies. Oil of erigeron is reported to work immediately for controlling light flea infestations. Sprays and cleaning solutions containing citrus oil are believed to have flea-repelling properties.

Herbal Flea Collars. These cotton collars, sometimes refillable (or rechargeable), may contain pennyroyal and other herbs, including citronella, eucalyptus, spearmint, cedar, orange, and rue. Herbal flea collars may make your pet smell better, but there's unfortunately little evidence to suggest that they'll offer more than a slight amount of protection against fleas.

Pyrethrin. There are many flea sprays that contain pyrethrin, a natural pesticide derived from pyrethrum daisies. You can apply these sprays directly to your pets. But use pyrethrin sprays only as a last resort and be sure to strictly follow the directions on the label. Some animals are very allergic to pyrethrins, so watch your pet carefully after application. If you any notice skin redness or itching, wash off the spray immediately and contact your veterinarian to see if any further medication will be required. Some synthetic formulations such as per-methrin are extremely toxic to cats, so read product labels carefully and don't use anything on your cat unless it's specifically labeled for that purpose.

A Mouse in the House.

If you see one mouse, chances are there are plenty more unseen, since these rodents are incredibly fertile and prolific. One female mouse might give birth to as many as 60 mice in a single year. The key is to inspect all potential entryways into your home, and keep out mice (and other pests as well!) by patching, filling holes, and making sure openings close tightly. Here's a partial list of potential trouble spots to scrutinize.

- Check the garage, specifically the garage door. Make sure the seal on the bottom of the door is intact and free from holes and gaps.
- Inspect all the openings where anything passes through the wall: dryer vents, phone lines, cable TV lines, electric lines, etc.
- Look for small holes or openings in and around window and roof vent screens.
- Examine the fascia and soffit for holes.
- Check for holes in the foundation mortar.
- Seek out any gaps between foundation and siding, and seal thoroughly with caulk.
- Make sure shrub and tree branches don't touch the house, and stack your wood away from the house.

If mice do come in, the safest, surest, most humane way to deal with them is with a snap trap. Set two traps end-to-end with the baited ends out along the baseboard and bait them with chocolate, peanut butter, or nuts. For best results, bait the traps without setting them, and allow the mice to steal the bait a few times. Then when you do set the traps, the mice will be more likely to bite.

PART 2

AROUND THE SUBURBAN YARD

GARAGES AND DRIVEWAYS

Time cotton rags take to biodegrade:

What's in your garage? Besides the car—if it still fits—you probably have the usual assortment of bikes, power equipment, tools, toys, and other stuff. It's the other stuff that can get scary: used paint thinner, half a bottle of gas additive, maybe even some old pesticides left by a previous owner.

Sensible Storage or Toxic Dump? The garage is where all of the "outdoor" stuff takes refuge from the elements. Anything that's too big, too messy, and/or too smelly to go in the house winds up in the garage. Dad's power tools, Mom's gardening equipment, oil and gas for cars and mowers, spray almost always end up in the garage, never to be reopened. Instead of stockpiling it in your garage, how should you really get rid of old paint? First, see if anybody else wants it—try to give it to someone who can use it. If that doesn't work, find something to paint. Using up paint is the best way to get rid of it.

1 to 5 months. Time cigarette butts take to biodegrade: 1 to 12 years.

for the roses, partial gallons of old paint, oily rags, lawn chairs, ladders, and more: Anything goes out there. There are mason jars of mystery liquids tucked away on the back of shelves. There are chemistry experiments in progress on the workbench. There's sawdust on the floor and the smell of grease in the air. Problem is, a lot of the stuff found in the garage is not exactly green. And some of it is quite toxic. All of it should be handled with care.

Putting Old Paint Out to Pasture. Chances are, there are some cans of paint on a shelf somewhere in the garage. No matter how carefully you measure and estimate, every painting project seems to leave behind a partial can or two. And those drip-spattered cans

Post-Painting Cleanup

You need only soap and water to clean latex paint from bushes and rollers. Clean them in a sink, not over a storm drain. Never use gasoline to clean paint brushes used in oil-based paint; use turpentine or odorless mineral spirits.

GARAGES AND DRIVEWAYS

If that paint is latex- or water-based, and there's just a little bit left, open the can and let it dry in the sun. Once the paint has solidified, you can toss the can in the trash for regular waste collection.. Or, apply the remaining paint to a piece of scrap wood, allow it to dry, and toss that in the trash.

Oil-based paints are another more toxic story because of the solvents in them. Dispose of leftover oil-based paints—and any paint that you suspect contains lead—at a household hazardous waste facility. To find a disposal site, contact your local Cooperative Extension office, your municipal recycling or waste management office, or the landfill or waste transfer station that serves your area.

Take care with paint rags, too. Rags soaked in oil-based paint or solvents are fire hazards. They can ignite spontaneously, so store them in tightly sealed cans until you can dispose of them. Do not throw them out with the trash; instead, take them to a hazardous waste facility. It's okay to toss out rags used with latex paint. Just make sure they're thoroughly dry, and wrap them in newspaper before tossing them.

By buying the right paint, you can solve the disposal problem in advance. Choose latex paint over oil-based paint whenever possible. Even better, choose new solvent-free latex paints, sometimes called low-VOC or low-odor paints.

Stay Away from Strippers. Your parents probably didn't mean paint strippers when they told you to stay away from strippers, but it was good advice all the same. Unless you listened (not likely), there's probably half a can of paint thinner or stripper tucked away on a shelf.

Thinners and strippers contain almost 100 percent solvents, and all solvents are poisonous. Even inhalation or absorption can have serious health consequences, including eye, nose, and throat irritation, and damage to your internal organs and nerves. The most hazardous classes of solvents are the aromatic and chlorinated hydrocarbons, such as benzene, toluene, xylene, and methylene chloride.

Given the choice, choose products with the less hazardous nonchlorinated solvents, such as isopropanol (rubbing alcohol), ethanol (grain alcohol), acetone (nail polish remover), and turpentine.

Even better advice: Don't buy thinners or strippers at all. Use latex paint so you don't need thinners. Instead of strippers, remove paint manually by scraping or sandpapering. If that seems like too

More Solvent Safety

While you're exercising caution in your solvent choices and handling, add these safety practices to your repertoire.

• Don't refuel the mower or power tools in the garage. You're at greater risk of inhaling benzene and other solvents while in confined spaces.

• Keep several funnels in the garage to use when filling the mower with gasoline or adding oil to your car. If you don't have a funnel handy and need to add oil, use an unwaxed paper cup with a pencil hole poked in the bottom.

Time a plastic six-pack ring takes to biodegrade: 450 years.

GARAGES AND DRIVEWAYS

much work, look for one of the new generation of paint removers that do not contain volatile solvents. One example is "Safest Stripper" by 3M.

No matter what you choose, never pour solvents down the drain or into the ground. The only safe way to dispose of unwanted solvents is to take them to a household hazardous waste collection site.

New Ways for Driveways. The suburbs, of course, are built around the automobile. And the car has its own place of honor on every lot—the driveway. We don't give these asphalt wastelands much thought, but they take up a lot of space, they alter the environment, they waste a ton of water, and they're ugly to boot.

Suburban Hot Spots. The air temperature over an asphalt or concrete driveway can be 20° to 40°F higher in summer than over a neighboring patch of grass. And unlike a lawn, which accepts rainwater and cycles it through the soil, the driveway sheds water, sending it directly into the storm sewer. Often, that water carries with it traces of motor oil, gasoline, and other automotive waste. Every time an inch of rain falls, more than ½ gallon of water per square foot of driveway washes off into the sewer.

Asphalt Alternatives. So what can you do instead? Concrete is no better than asphalt. Grass alone just doesn't work; it won't take the stress of being driven over and parked on. And dirt? Too messy. Gravel is somewhat better. It allows for a bit of water penetration and doesn't elevate temperatures as much. However, gravel requires regular maintenance.

There is a better way. What if you could have the benefits of a lawn and pavement together? You can with a clever new solution, called turf pavers. These concrete cell grids have hollow middles in which grass can be planted. (Think of a latticed crust on a blueberry pie.) The concrete, flush with the ground, supports traffic. The grass grows to hide the concrete. The grids are easy to install and are a good choice if you're starting a driveway from scratch. Or, you can also experiment with making your own turf pavers simply by laying regular concrete pavers with enough spacing to allow grass to grow between them.

Either way, you'll need to plant a tough grass, like perennial ryegrass or bermudagrass, that will stand up to traffic. It will also require more maintenance—especially additional watering—than a regular lawn.

And you'll have to find somewhere else to put up the basketball hoop.

Natural Icebreakers. No matter how hot
your driveway gets in the summer, it's bound to seek the other extreme when winter rolls around. Most of us can stand the cold. Snow, even lots of it, has its charm. But ice that's not on a skating rink is another

Safer Sealer

Most folks aren't going to give up their asphalt driveway, so they'll still engage in the biennial ritual of sealing. They'll choose the hottest day of the year, haul out the big buckets of coal tar and squeegees, and start spreading sealant on the driveway. This infernal practice is a necessary evil, since sealing helps prevent the elements from cracking and crumbling the driveway surface. But if you're leery of spreading coal tar on your driveway, there is an easier, safer, albeit more expensive remedy—100 percent acrylic driveway sealer. It costs more than coal tar and other kinds of sealers, but a smaller quantity spreads over a far greater area and it lasts longer. If you live in California, don't even bother to look for coal tar—it has been taken off the market in response to concerns about its negative environmental effects.

story, especially when it's clinging to steps, sidewalks, and driveways. So we follow tradition and pour on the salt to make the ice go away. Then, come spring, we scratch our heads and wonder why the grass is brown or the perennials are stunted. The reason is . . . salt. Sure, it melts the snow, but it can also leave a lot of dead and damaged plants in its wake—to say nothing of the salt that washes off into sewers and groundwater.

What did the ancient Corinthians do when they wanted to devastate the land of the cities they conquered? They spread salt on the earth. What do we do when we want to melt ice from our driveways, sidewalks, and steps? We spread salt—sodium chloride. And the result, although not quite as devastating, is similar. The salt washes off the walk or drive and into the surrounding soil, where it damages or even kills turf and foundation plants, perennials, and anything else that happens to have its roots in that salty soil. In time, the salt actually eats away at the concrete of steps and sidewalks.

The alternative doesn't have to be a skating rink for cars or a nasty spill on your steps. But there are more environmentally friendly ways to rid steps and sidewalks of dangerous ice.

Ice Melters. You can find so-called landscape-friendly ice melters in some catalogs and at home centers. Generally, their active ingredient is urea fertilizer. Although this chemical fertilizer is not as harsh as salt, it still may burn plants and leach into the groundwater. Better to use a fertilizer such as calcium nitrate that's not quite as potent. Even better, use alfalfa meal, a totally natural fertilizer that contains nitrogen to promote ice melting and has a texture to provide traction while it works.

HOW TO

Clean Up Your Concrete

Does your concrete driveway, patio, or garage floor look worn and dingy? You can clean it without using dangerous chemicals if you mix up your own all-purpose concrete cleaner.

¼ cup of washing soda (available at supermarkets)
2 gallons of warm water

Mix the water and soda together. Wash concrete using a brush. Rinse with water. If that doesn't work, you can revitalize a worn, dingy concrete driveway by coating it with a self-bonding concrete resurfacer, such as Top 'n Bond. Special additives allow it to bond well with existing concrete. Apply a layer no more than ½ inch thick. To patch concrete that has deeper cracks and holes, use standard crack mix.

Traction Helpers. For just plain traction, cover ice with wood ashes, coal cinders, sand, or cat litter.

Slip Stoppers. Invest in some non-slip stair treads for your favorite slippery steps.

Fire and Ice. For fast ice relief, fire up a propane weed torch, and melt the ice in a hurry. Just make sure that there's someplace for the water to drain, or you'll just be moving the problem to another site.

The American dream has four wheels. It's parked right outside the house or in the garage, its own special house. It's new, and it's shiny, and it takes us wherever we want to go. Nothing exemplifies the American success story more than the automobile—preferably a new one every 3 or 4 years.

The Environmental Cost of a Car. As much as we love our cars, and as much as living in the suburbs is about driving just about everywhere we go, owning (and driving) automobiles is our single most damaging environmental act. Conversely, the single best environmental act is a nonact: refraining from buying that new car.

Most of us have some idea of the pollutants that are released and the environmental damage that is done by a typical car. Every year, it spews more than 10,000 pounds of carbon dioxide and other pollutants into the air. Light trucks and the ever-popular sport-utility vehicles (SUVs) are even worse, emitting up to 60 percent more of each. Multiply that by a vehicle's 10-year life span, and that's a lot of dirty air.

Even if we are aware of the damage caused by driving a vehicle, we tend to overlook the environmental cost of making one. Just building that car creates over 700 pounds of pollutants and 8,000 pounds of carbon dioxide. And there are the tons of raw materials consumed as well.

So every time you don't buy a car, you're making the air a bit cleaner. And if that car you're not buying would have been an additional, second car, you're avoiding even more pollution.

Of course, trying to squeeze another year out of your old car makes eco-sense only if it's not an exhaust-spewing, gas-guzzling heap. (In general, if your car gets fewer than 20 miles to the gallon, it would be better to trade it in for a more efficient new or used model.) But no matter what you're driving, you need to keep it in good running order.

Stay in Tune. Don't scrimp when it comes to tune-ups and regular maintenance. Follow the manufacturer's guidelines and have tune-ups done as recommended. A poorly tuned engine with old spark plugs will produce as much as 25 percent more carbon monoxide and 16 percent more nitrogen oxides than a well-tuned one.

The number of motor vehicles in the world

Open the Windows. Use your car's air conditioner sparingly, and replace air-conditioning hoses every 3 years to prevent the escape of ozone-layer–destroying coolants into the atmosphere.

CARS

more than doubled between 1970 and 1985.

During the 1990s, the automobile growth rate was three times the human population growth rate.

CARS

Slow Down. Fuel economy decreases by 2 percent for every mile over 55 mph. Aggressive driving habits such as jack-rabbit acceleration or excessive speed can increase fuel consumption by as much as 50 percent and generate 100 times as much carbon monoxide and hydrocarbon emissions.

Park and Walk. You know that puff of smoke that shoots from the tailpipe when you start the car? That's a poisonous stew of nitrogen oxides, hydrocarbons, and carbon dioxide. Cold starts cause your car to emit the most pollutants. The fewer times you start (and stop) your engine during the day, the less you pollute. Trying walking to lunch or to the store.

Pump It Up. Check the air pressure of your tires monthly to make sure they are inflated according to the manufacturer's recommendations. It's estimated that underinflated tires waste 2 million gallons of gas in the United States every day!

Check the Pipes. Check your car's exhaust system annually. Make sure the muffler and catalytic converter are leak-free and working properly.

TIPS

Skip the Scary Solvents

Do not use engine degreasers, engine cleaners, or tire cleaners. They all contain harmful solvents that get rinsed off your car and into groundwater and sewers.

CARS

Stay Sleek and Streamlined. Improve fuel efficiency by removing temporary roof racks when they're not needed. Don't haul unnecessary weight that will make your car's engine work harder.

Lighten Up. Finally, if you must venture into the showroom, know your MPGs (miles per gallon). Use a resource such as the Environmental Defense Fund's *Green Car: A Guide to Cleaner Vehicle Production, Use, and Disposal;* the American Council for an Energy-Efficient Economy's *Green Book: The Environmental Guide to Cars and Trucks;* or the U.S. Department of Energy's Fuel Economy site (see "Resources" on page 151 for Internet addresses). These will help you select the most fuel-efficient vehicle. And shop for a low-emission car. If most of your driving is done in an urban environment, consider a hybrid gasoline/electric vehicle. Look for a car with a high aluminum content, too. It's lighter, and much of the raw material may have been recycled.

Natural Car Care.

Few things make a person feel like a responsible car owner quite as much as changing the oil in his car. Unfortunately, home oil changes all too often involve home oil spills. And it doesn't take very much spilled oil to cause a problem. One gallon of used motor oil—about as much as is generated in a single oil change—has the potential to contaminate up to 1 million gallons of water. So, if you're going to do that oil change yourself, be very careful about spills, drain the oil into a container that has a tight-fitting lid, and take the used oil to an approved disposal center for recycling.

You can turn in the used oil filter to a collection center, as well. Just make sure to drain the oil from the filter for at least 12 hours before recycling it.

TIPS

Use a Safer Antifreeze

Use an antifreeze that contains propylene glycol rather than ethylene glycol. Ethylene glycol antifreeze is toxic to pets and wildlife, even if they consume just a little bit of it. Even propylene glycol antifreeze needs to be disposed of properly after it's been used, to avoid contaminating soil and water with traces of lead and gasoline that may collect in the antifreeze.

If you do happen to spill, clean up conscientiously. On concrete or asphalt, soak up spilled oil with rags or cat litter, and wash the area with mild cleanser. On dirt or gravel, dig up the contaminated area. Take oil-contaminated rags, soil, gravel, or cat litter to an oil recycling center or to a hazardous waste disposal facility for proper disposal.

Old Oil as Good as New. What happens to that oil once it's returned to the collection center? It gets recycled, so it can be reused. Oil doesn't wear out. It just gets dirty. Once it's re-refined (or recycled), it's as good as new. The oil is cleaned, and additives that have been used up are added back into the oil to bring it up to the same quality as virgin oil. That process takes about one-third of the energy that's needed to refine virgin oil. Is it safe? You bet. Re-refined oil earns the seal of approval from the American Petroleum Institute (API), and using any API-certified oil, re-refined included, keeps your warranty intact. Hard to find? Nope. You'll find it at many Napa Auto Parts stores.

More than 10 million vehicles are scrapped every year in the United States.

CARS

HOW TO

Put a Shine on Your Jalopy

Once the oil has been changed, it's time to make the outside of the car sparkle. But you don't need to use harsh cleansers to get it looking good. Here's a recipe for a safe, gentle car cleanser that will make the old sedan shine. In a 5-gallon bucket combine:

½ cup of white vinegar
½ cup of baby shampoo

Fill the bucket with warm water, and apply to the car with a soft sponge. Rinse.

If baby shampoo's not a staple in your home or if you'd rather not mix your own solution, you can find environmentally friendly car cleansers from mail-order and Internet sources. Look for products that are free of solvents and harsh chemicals.

For heavy grime, road grease, and tar, make a paste by mixing baking soda with a small amount of warm water. Scrub using a soft-bristled brush. Rinse.

If summertime watering restrictions put a crimp in your home car-washing routine, plan a stop by your local automatic car wash instead. Most of these businesses recycle their wash water to keep waste to a minimum.

The first automobile ad appeared on TV in 1946.

DECKS AND WALKWAYS

If the current rate of deforestation continues, the world's rain forests will vanish within 100 years.

In the suburbs, we cling to our little rafts of wooden planks, surrounded by a sea of grass. Those rafts are our decks, where we gather to eat, to entertain, to relax. The deck has replaced the front porch as the family gathering place.

Hit the Deck Running. Our decks get used and abused. They get scratched and faded. They crack and rot. And they require a lot of maintenance. There's the staining, the weatherproofing, the repairing, and the painting. All that work demands that we make sensible environmental choices.

Those choices begin with the wood itself. There are plenty of options, even after we reject pressure-treated CCA (chromium copper arsenate) wood, as we must. There's no question that CCA-treated wood is the wrong choice for a deck. Just think about standing on, eating from, and watching the kids crawl along a deck that has been soaked with arsenic and chromium. You could call it the deck of a sinking ship.

That arsenic and those other compounds are not entirely stable in the wood. They may rub off on skin or leach out into soil and groundwater. And working with and disposing of wood that's been treated with these toxic compounds is especially dangerous. Still, pressure-treated CCA lumber remains, unfortunately, the decking of choice across the country.

Fortunately, there are good alternatives. For pressure-treated wood, there is a new treatment called ACQ (alkaline copper quat) that uses no arsenic or chromium. Although this type of wood treatment does contain copper, which can be toxic to earthworms and aquatic life, it's much better for the earth and for your health than CCA. However, ACQ is also more expensive and is still hard to find in some areas; look for products such as ACQ Preserve or Preserve Plus. The best choice is naturally rot-resistant wood or, believe it or not, plastic-wood hybrids.

Homegrown Rot-Resistant Woods. A few years ago, redwood was a big no-no for anyone who cared about the environment because venerable old-growth trees were laying down their lives to become lawn furniture. Today, redwood is a renewable resource, as millions of redwood seedlings are replanted every year—about five for every tree harvested. And cedar is an even better choice since it can be forested even more easily and quickly than redwood.

Both native woods are naturally rot-resistant. They are good, reasonable, nonchemical alternatives to pressure-treated wood, but they are not totally care-free, and a deck made from either redwood or cedar will still require regular maintenance.

DECKS AND WALKWAYS

Make Wise Wood Buys. There are many different standards for both redwood and cedar. Sapwood, the part nearest the bark, will rot when exposed to moisture. For redwood decking, the best choice is "kiln-dried deck heart" or "deck common." Less durable (but still acceptable) for decks are "clear heart," "clear," "B heart," and "B grade redwood." For the longest-lasting cedar deck, choose "clear all-heart cedar." Less reliable—but still an okay low-cost alternative for dry climates—is "grade No. 1 select tight knot (STK)."

These types of wood may be two or three times as expensive as pressure-treated wood. For example, "B grade redwood" starts at about $5 per square foot; "kiln-dried deck heart" costs much more.

Tropical Wood Alternatives. There are other rot-resistant woods that are just coming to the American market, including ipe (also known as ironwood) and cambara. These exotic woods will last for 20 years or more with just one preservative treatment. However, they are expensive, hard to find, and very difficult to work with. Ask to see certification of sustainable harvesting methods before you buy any tropical wood products.

Perhaps Plastic. Plastic has hit the deck and, in some cases, it looks better than you might imagine. Believe it or not, plastic decking may be the best choice in terms of the environment. Aesthetically, well, that's a different matter. New wood composites are a blend of 30 to 50 percent recycled plastic or plastic resins with wood fibers. These extruded products are virtually indestructible, while resisting rot, insects, and UV rays. Composite lumber weathers to a light gray and can be painted or stained, and protective sealers aren't required. Some brands do have a plastic look to them; others closely resemble natural wood. Surface texturing produces a wood-grain look and feel. Do you want this stuff hanging off the back of your house? You'll have to shop around, take a look, and judge for yourself.

Dealing with Your Deck.
Old or new, wood or whatever, if you have a deck, it's in your best interest to maintain it. For starters, keep it clean. Regular sweeping rids the deck of leaves and other yard debris that keep the wood moist and prone to decay.

Seal It. Although they're rot-resistant, even redwood and cedar require regular treatment with a water repellant or sealer. These sealants rely on wax and/or polyurethane to prevent water from entering and damaging the wood. Look for water-based rather than solvent-based sealants. Apply at deck construction (but not during wet weather), and reapply every 2 years. Most sealants are semitransparent, but some contain light stains. Water repellants do not, however, keep the wood from turning gray—that's caused by the sun's UV rays, not by water.

Renew It. The sun's UV rays break down the wood's cells, and cause the characteristic fade-to-gray color of redwood and cedar. Think of it as a sort of sunburn—a microscopically thin layer of burnt fibers on the surface of the wood—that darkens the wood.

To restore, apply a deck or wood "brightener" to remove dirt, stains, and gray wood fibers. But most include chlorine bleach among their ingredients. It's better to shop for a cleaner that contains a nonbleach

The wood preservative pentachlorophenol has been linked to cirrhosis of the liver, bone

marrow atrophy, and nervous disorders.

whitener (such as sodium percarbonate) or peroxide. Scrub the deck to remove the gray wood, and rinse. After the wood has dried, you can apply a clear finish. This will keep the wood from drying out, cracking, or rotting, but it won't prevent fading. Like the graying of America, the graying of our decks is inevitable.

Stain It. Once it's sealed, your deck won't require a repeat waterproofing treatment for 3 years. You can also forestall fading by applying an exterior stain that will keep your deck bright and waterproof for about 4 years. There are several good-quality deck stains available that are based on water rather than solvents. Paint requires the least maintenance of all. Coat your deck with a latex paint, and it will be care-free, except for washing down, for 7 to 8 years. Which leaves you plenty of time to attend to your other yard chores.

Pave Your Own Way. Usually the scruffiest

part of the lawn is the path everyone travels—to get to the back door, shed, garden, or pool. So maybe it's time to give up on grass and make it an official path that incorporates some sort of durable material. But

HOW TO

Make Concrete Stepping Stones

Why not make your own custom stepping stones for that path? Concrete stepping stones are easy to make, and they are surprisingly good-looking.

One cardboard Sonotube concrete footing form, available at most home centers
Concrete mix
Heavy-duty plastic sheeting (4- to 6-mil)
Peat moss (optional)
Marbles, stones, jewels (optional)

1. Mix concrete per directions on the bag. (For a more natural and rough look, add 2 handfuls of dry peat moss to 5 gallons of mixed concrete.)
2. With a hacksaw, cut several 1- to 1½-inch-wide radial slices from the Sonotube.
3. Lay the tubes on a plastic sheet on a flat surface and fill them with concrete.
4. Let the concrete set until nearly dry, then cut and peel off the cardboard Sonotube.
5. Before the concrete sets thoroughly, you can decorate the surface of the stepping-stone with stones, marbles, or anything you desire by pressing them into the surface of the concrete. For fun, decorate stepping stones to commemorate birthdays and other special occasions. When you're finished, your concrete creations will have a look that's uniquely yours.

what can you use that's easy and inexpensive, and that reflects your own creativity? Not gravel; it's too industrial-looking. Bricks are nice, but perhaps too formal, and a brick path requires a lot of work to lay it properly and to maintain it. Pavers from the home center are just too, well . . . suburban. Try paving your own way using low-cost, readily available materials. You may be able to get free wood chips from your local yard waste drop-off site. If you have access to a fallen tree, saw off 2-inch-thick slices of trunk to make neat, natural stepping stones.

Nothing defines a suburban summer evening like food searing over a charcoal fire. Ahh, the smell of lighter fluid in the air, the cloud of billowing smoke as hot fat hits blazing coals. No one would claim that barbecuing the 1950s way is healthy, but who wants to give it up?

Natural Barbecue. Traditional barbecuing methods may not be healthy, but the good news is that we don't have to abandon treasured rituals like summer cookouts. We just need to adjust in our technique to keep the pleasures while eliminating the health hazards of open-fire cooking.

There's No Fuel Like an Old Fuel. First, consider the coals. Most traditional barbecuers opt for the convenience of charcoal briquettes. Those uniform pillows of charcoal are inexpensive and readily available. They also burn longer and more uniformly than old-fashioned lump hardwood charcoal. But there is a price to pay for that convenience. Briquettes are not pure charcoal. Instead, they consist of charcoal dust held together with various fillers, which may include sawdust, cardboard, limestone, and even motor oil.

Briquettes are also more difficult to light than hardwood charcoal. That's why some instant briquettes have been impregnated with petrochemical charcoal lighter fluid. Although the smell—and the chemicals—theoretically burn off by the time the briquettes are fully ignited, you're still releasing chemical fumes into the air. Better to use hardwood charcoal for the pure and unadulterated wood flavor. Or, if you prefer the convenience of briquettes, you can sometimes find natural briquettes that contain only vegetable starches as filler.

Try a Natural Light. Many of us have enjoyed the guilty thrill of squeezing a can of charcoal lighter fluid as flames leap from the coals. There is indeed a dramatic appeal to chemically saturated coals roaring into flame. But is that little bit of theater worth inhaling (and perhaps ingesting) something akin to kerosene? No, not when you don't have to. And you really don't have to. Not when there are much better, safer, and even easier ways to start a charcoal fire in the outdoor barbeque.

These days you have plenty of choices when it comes to fire starting.

Electric fire starter. Just plug it into an outlet and bury the element in a mountain of coals, and in no time you have a red-hot fire.

In 1950, the typical beer can weighed in

OUTDOOR ENTERTAINING

at a hefty 91 grams. By 1990 it had slimmed down to 17 grams.

HOW TO

Fight Grill Flare-Ups (and Cancer)

Where there's smoke, there's fire. And where there's fire (on a grill), there are often hetero-cyclic amines. These potentially carcinogenic compounds are created in the charred meat that results when fat drips onto coals, causing the fire to flare up and burn meat on the grill. Health concerns aside, good barbecuers want to prevent those flare-ups, if only for the sake of flavor. That's why some grill chefs spend their time with a squirt bottle of water in hand, trying to dampen the raging fire. There's a much easier way. You can completely elimi-nate flare-ups by using a drip pan and cooking slowly over even heat.

   To grill with a drip pan you'll need:

A large grill, preferably with a lid
A pan, which can be as simple and inexpensive
   as an aluminum pie plate

1. Before lighting the coals, place the drip pan in the center of the charcoal grate, and sur-round it with a layer of charcoal.
2. Light the coals, put the grill in place, and place the meat directly over the pan.
3. As the meat cooks, the fat and grease will drip into the pan and not onto the coals; there-fore, no flare-ups. However, since the heat is indirect, cooking will take longer, perhaps half again as much time as with direct cooking.

Time an aluminum can takes to biodegrade: 80 to 100 years.

Paraffin block. Put two or three of these cubes in with the coals, light, and they will burn long enough to ignite the charcoal.

Fire-starting chimney. This ingenious device may be the best fire-starter of all. Based on the old Boy Scout coffee-can fire starter, it's a metal cylinder with vent holes, an insulated handle, and a screen. Crumple three sheets of newspaper and stuff them into the bottom, fill the top with charcoal, light the newspaper, and, within 20 minutes, the coals are

HOW TO

Slow Cookin' with Gas

Indirect slow cooking is even easier on a gas grill because, unlike a charcoal grill, you don't have to shove coals around or refuel in the middle of cooking. To slow cook on a gas grill:

1. Turn all burners to high and preheat for 5 minutes.
2. Turn one burner off.
3. Place a drip pan over that burner.
4. Turn the other burner(s) down to medium.
5. Place meat over the drip pan.
6. Close the lid.
7. Resist the urge to check constantly. Opening the lid adds 5 minutes to the cooking time.

red-hot. Simply grab the chimney by the handles and overturn it to dump the coals into the grill. The chimney is especially useful if you're roasting a whole chicken, turkey, or anything that requires hours of heat, as you can start a second batch of coals as the first dies down.

HOW TO

Make a Coffee-Can Charcoal Chimney

It's easy to fashion your own fire-starting chimney from an empty 2- or 3-pound coffee can.

1. With a can opener, punch six or eight holes into the side of the can along the can's bottom edge.
2. Remove the bottom of the can.
3. Place the can in the grill and stuff three sheets of crumpled newspaper in the bottom of the can.
4. Carefully fill the can with charcoal.
5. Insert a lighted match through the holes along the bottom of the can to light the newspaper. The newspaper will slowly burn up, igniting the charcoal. In about 20 minutes, the coals will be red-hot. Use long-handled tongs to lift the can, leaving the coals on the grill. Then set the can aside—but remember, it's hot, too. Don't just drop it on the grass.

You can also make a chimney from a ½-gallon milk carton. Cut out the bottom, place just one sheet of crumpled newspaper in it, then fill with charcoal and light.

Bocce and Beyond.

Our backyards are grown-up versions of the playgrounds of our youth. They are wide-open grassy spaces where we and our families can gather to have fun. Too often, though, they're underused and neglected. Sure, our yards might host an occasional game of pitch-and-catch or touch football, but that's usually about it.

Lay in a few sporting supplies and put that sunny expanse to good use. Start with a bocce set and a tube of the chalk used to mark athletic fields. To create a more "official" looking field for your backyard bocce games, measure out a rectangular playing court that's 10 to 15 feet wide and 60 to 95 feet long. Mark the boundaries with chalk and let the bocce begin.

A volleyball and associated net make good use of grassy spaces as will a set of croquet mallets. If your lawn is a bit small for volleyball or bocce, drive in a couple of stakes for horseshoe pitching. Maybe you'll never host Wimbledon in your backyard, but there are certainly plenty of gently athletic options to attract activity to your outdoor areas.

'Skeeter Beaters.

Fortunately or unfortunately, you and your family aren't the only life forms frolicking in your yard. A healthy, organic landscape also receives visits from birds, squirrels, and other critters, and hosts its fair share of insects, too—including mosquitoes. Few things can take the pleasure out of a picnic as quickly as a buzzing, biting cloud of blood-sucking mosquitoes. Formerly recognized as mere nuisances, these pests now inspire fear, given their potential to carry diseases such as the West Nile virus. What's a homeowner to do? For that matter, what's anyone to do?

It costs over $300 per year to maintain an acre of home lawn.

Watching your family and friends playing croquet in the haze of one of those pesticide foggers isn't (and never was) a good option—the health risks associated with those easily inhaled products are greater than the odds of being bitten by a disease-bearing mosquito. In the summers of 1999 and 2000, nearly half of New York City was doused from the air with malathion—a supposedly "safe" insecticide—in an attempt to control mosquitoes carrying West Nile virus. But malathion, the number-one mosquito killer since good old "safe" DDT was removed from the shelves, is a nerve toxin; acute exposure can cause headaches, dizziness, blurred vision, and difficult breathing. Meanwhile, millions of people may have been exposed to this chemical, and it didn't wipe out the mosquitoes anyway.

Short of staying indoors all summer, there aren't any ways to guarantee that mosquitoes won't put the bite on you. Following are ways to reduce your risk of being bitten and some popular mosquito control and repellent methods that aren't really as good as they seem.

Bug Zappers. The eerie green glow and electric *zzzt* of bug zappers are common suburban sights and sounds. They may add to the atmosphere in the evening, but they don't do much to control their targeted pest: mosquitoes. These zappers kill far more moths and beneficial insects than mosquitoes. In fact, a recent study showed that over a 2-month period, six backyard bug zappers killed a total of 13,789 insects. Only 31 of them were mosquitoes or other biting insects. Far more of the zapped insects were beneficials that feed on mosquitoes and other pests. In fact, zappers are banned in Germany because of their threat to beneficials.

Zappers don't work because they rely on ultraviolet light to attract insects, and ultraviolet light is not what mosquitoes zero in on. However, there is a new generation of zappers, led by the Dragonfly, that emit three powerful skeeter attractants: CO_2, octenol, and heat. These improved zappers can attract and kill thousands of mosquitoes in a single night. And they do it without spraying exploded insect parts all over the deck. The same company also markets a small fogger that releases citronella and other masking scents to confuse mosquitoes and keep them from biting.

Chemical Repellents. How badly do you want to avoid being bitten? Virtually all mainstream mosquito repellents contain DEET (diethyl toluamide) in amounts varying from 10 percent to 100 percent. DEET is also the product that is most often recommended for successfully repelling ticks. But read the label. It cautions that DEET is hazardous and should not come in contact with eyes, mouth, or even skin. There are lots of warnings about using it on young children. In fact, DEET has been implicated as one of a combination of chemicals that may be a cause of Gulf War syndrome, symptoms of which include painful joints, tingling and numbness in the hands and feet, muscle fatigue, and pain.

Natural Repellants. Natural bug repellants usually contain oil of citronella, and sometimes other fragrant herbs. They work (to some degree) by masking human scent. The higher the citronella content, the more effective they are. Most sprays and candles contain ½ percent citronella by volume. But for best results, look for products that contain 1 to 2 percent. Keep in mind that when mosquitoes are within 30 feet of their target, they rely on sight as well as scent, so scented repellants are not effective if you are in or near a wooded area that's heavily populated with mosquitoes.

Break Their Breeding Habits. The best way to clear an area of mosquitoes is to keep them from breeding, or to kill their larvae before they mature. Where do they breed? In still water. And it doesn't have to be a lot. It could be a pond, a birdbath, or an old tire that's filled with water. Hunt down and eliminate standing water. If there's water you can't or don't want to get rid of, you can use mosquito control rings to release BTI (*Bacillus thuringiensis* var. *israelensis*), a natural bacterial mosquito larvae killer, in the water. Each rings treats 100 square feet of surface area and lasts for 30 days. That should be plenty of time to hold a bite-free barbecue or two.

Every year 45,000 people are poisoned by

pesticides in the United States.

SWIMMING POOLS

A swimming pool filter consumes nearly

With all of the health and environmental hazards associated with chlorine, you would think that diving into a tub of it is the last thing someone would want to do. Yet millions of people do it—and call it healthy recreation.

The (Almost) Chemical-Free Pool. In a perfect world you could keep your backyard swimming pool water sparkling clean and safe without chlorine. Just look at the Olympics: At the 1996 Summer Games in Atlanta, the swimming pools were disinfected with ozone rather than chlorine. Of course, there weren't any kids having "accidents" in the Olympic pools. Our suburban swimming spots have to withstand a lot more use—and abuse.

We love to keep our pool water crystal clear. No one wants to swim in murky water that's crawling with algae and bacteria. And so most of us think that chlorine is a necessary—albeit undesirable—part of our pool-care regimen. While that may be partly true, there are pool treatments that will enable you to reduce the amount of chlorine that goes into your favorite "cement pond." And cutting back on chlorine use is good for you *and* the environment.

The next time you stock up on pool supplies, take a look at your water-treatment options—chemical, electrical, and otherwise. Besides chlorine, there is one

other chemical pool treatment that is safe and effective enough to have earned Environmental Protection Agency approval (see below). There are also alternative treatments that can keep your pool water clean with substantially less chlorine use. Choose a system or combination of treatments that suits your pool configuration and level of use, as well as your budget. Don't try to get by with a treatment system that's too small for your pool's capacity, and don't be fooled by overstated claims on unknown products. When in doubt, consult a pool professional and follow their recommendations. Bacteria, after all, are nothing to mess with, and a pool full of murky water is not a particularly inviting place to spend your leisure time.

Chemical, but Not Chlorine. If you'd like to bypass chlorine altogether, take a look at biguanide (polyhexamethylene biguanide, or PHMB), a disinfectant that's actually more effective than chlorine—without the toxic drawbacks. Registered by the EPA for swimming pool use in 1982, biguanide, commonly available as Baquacil, does offer convenience and freedom from chlorine. But biguanide may cause pool water to foam, it's more expensive than chlorine,

twice as much electricity as a refrigerator.

and you'll also need to use a nonchlorine algicide and periodic "shock" doses of hydrogen peroxide. Some biguanide users have found that over a period of 6 to 8 years, some pool bacteria develop resistance to this water treatment regimen.

The problem with all of the other alternative treatments—ionizers, ozone generators, and UV filters—is that incomplete water circulation may leave patches of undisinfected water in the pool. That's why they are best used to supplement and reduce chlorine usage rather than to replace it entirely. These other treatment methods can also be used in combination with biguanide.

Ionizers. These futuristic machines work by passing low DC voltage through a set of metallic electrodes. This introduces atomic amounts of specific minerals into water, making it inhospitable to algae, bacteria, and certain other microorganisms sometimes found in pool water. In effect, it turns your pool water into mineral water. The mineral ions produced by the machines remain effective for weeks. The current is perfectly safe, and there is at least one solar-powered ionizer on the market. You'll still need a sophisticated filter to clean out debris. And you'll still need to use chlorine or biguanide on a regular basis.

The Centers for Disease Control and Prevention found that every bacterial

Ozone Generators. Many municipal water-treatment plants use ozone as a chlorine substitute. So if it's good enough to drink, it's good enough to swim in. Pool-size ozone generators use ultraviolet lamps to generate ozone, which kills microorganisms in the water. However, ozone is not 100 percent effective unless pH, temperature, and other water conditions are maintained at necessary levels. Maintaining those conditions perfectly is a job that most home owners are not equipped for. Supplemental chlorine may be needed. Or you can combine the ozone treatment process with biguanide, as was done at the Atlanta Olympics.

UV Filters. You can't see it, smell it, or taste it; it leaves no residue and contains no toxins, yet ultraviolet (UV) light is a powerful germicide. UV has been proven in municipal drinking-water-treatment facilities, where one 20-second exposure to UV light kills 99 percent of viruses and bacteria. Now it's possible to harness that power to clean the pool. Special UV pool filters push water through a chamber where it is exposed to high-frequency ultraviolet wavelengths capable of disrupting DNA and sterilizing microorganisms. The problem with UV filters is that if circulation is not complete, pockets of undisinfected water may remain. To play it safe, have the water tested regularly and be prepared to supplement with chlorine.

Check with your local pool and spa supply company about the availability and reliability of alternative water treatments. In the near future they may all be as effective as chlorine at preventing the growth of hazardous bacteria in your pool water.

Keep It Covered

Swimming pools are thirsty. It's mind-boggling to think of how much water pools use, even after they've been filled. For example, an average swimming pool in California loses $17\frac{1}{2}$ gallons of water per square foot of surface area per year. That's twice as much water as is required per square foot to maintain an orchard. Evaporation is the culprit. Like rust, it never sleeps, and it robs water that has to be replaced.

As we know from our junior-high science lessons, evaporation is a cooling process. That's why we sweat, remember? So evaporation cools the pool, too, lowering the temperature of the water, meaning more energy is required to heat it to a comfortable temperature. In all, evaporation accounts for as much as 70 percent of the energy lost by pools.

What's the answer? Keep the pool covered whenever it's not in use. Install an easy-to-operate cover so that you'll use it regularly.

Wind plays a role in energy loss, too, by aiding and abetting evaporation. A well-designed fence or hedge can help block the wind, further reducing water loss and energy expenditure.

outbreak in pools and spas during 1995 and 1996 was a result of undertreatment.

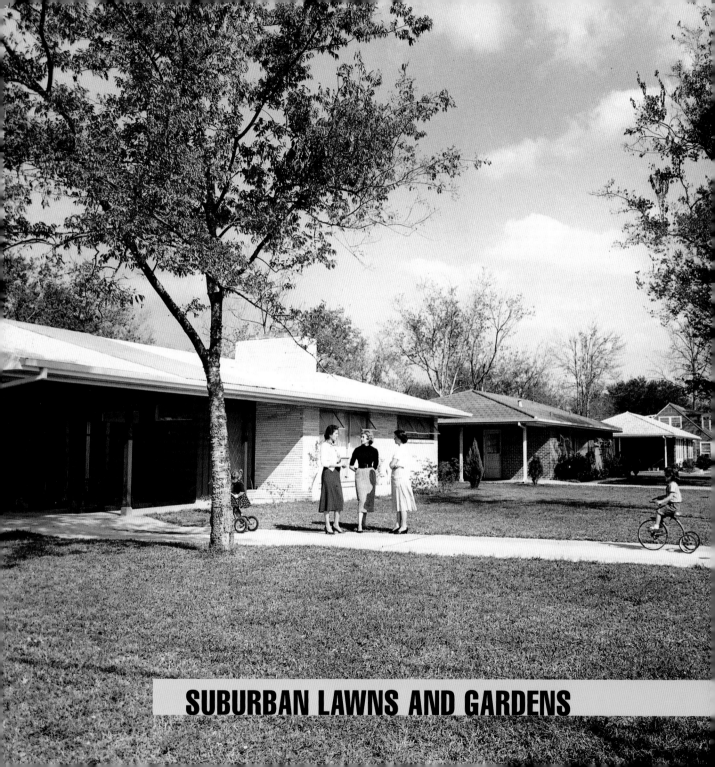

SUBURBAN LAWNS AND GARDENS

PART **3**

LAWN CARE

Americans spend an average of 40 hours per week tending their lawns.

The lawn is the tidy green fabric that knits the suburbs together. It's easy to become a slave to your lawn—endlessly mowing, trimming, weeding, and edging. But it's more fun to have an easy-care lawn that only looks like you spend a lot of time on it.

The Lawn, As You Like It. Although all lawns looked pretty much alike 30 or 40 years ago, today there's more of an opportunity to improvise and personalize your lawn. You can make that patch of grass reflect your personality. Here are few lawn looks to try on your own personal patch of America.

The Classic Lawn. If you're a traditionalist at heart, you might go for the retro, 1950s lawn. It's neat, trim, square-jawed—the perfect place for backyard barbecues and cutthroat croquet matches. Here's how to give your lawn an ultratidy classic look.

● Keep the edges sharp. Whenever you mow, use a foot-powered or rolling edger to trim along sidewalks and driveways. Install plastic edging along flowerbeds and around trees. Surround trees with mulch.

● Mow often. Frequent mowing keeps the lawn looking neat. That doesn't necessarily mean low mowing. High mowing puts less stress on your lawn, so it stays healthier. To maintain a 3-inch height, mow the grass before it reaches 4 inches tall.

● Ride herd on weeds. Use a long-handled turf weeder to pluck out dandelions and other invaders that would disrupt your lawn's precision look.

The Loose Lawn. Replace the lawn, or part of it, with an eco-lawn seed mix, consisting of tall-fescue turfgrass, plus herbs and flowers such as yarrow, English daisies, and clover. This turf will require less fertilizer, water, and mowing, but it will still serve the same purpose as a standard turfgrass lawn. You can purchase a commercial eco-lawn seed mix, or mix your own seed combination.

The Lesser Lawn. Want to do less mowing? Get less lawn. How? Shrink it. Gradually dig up the turf around the edges and replace it with groundcovers, wildflowers, or low-maintenance perennials. To speed and simplify the mowing that remains, smooth sharp corners into gentle curves.

The Low-Mow Lawn. Replace the lawn, or part of it, with a low-maintenance turfgrass species such as hard fescue or sheep fescue in the North, centipedegrass in the South, or buffalograss in the Plains and West. Although these grasses won't provide the look of a classic lawn, they will require much less maintenance.

The Stadium Lawn. If, when watching a baseball game on TV, you're more captivated by the striped outfield grass than the score, you're a candidate to stripe your own lawn. Making designs on a lawn can be a simple process if you have the right equipment—a reel mower and/or a lawn roller. You can make stripes by mowing with a reel in one direction and then back in the opposite. The mower blades and the roller behind them push the blades of grass

in opposite directions from one mowing pass to the next. As sunlight reflects on them, they appear as stripes. If you're using a rotary mower, follow up the mowing with alternating passes with an empty lawn roller to get your lawn in the ballpark.

Mow We Must. In a perfect world, we'd all have neat little lawns that could be maintained easily with an old-fashioned push reel mower, fueled only by our elbow grease, producing no emissions but our sweat, and silent but for the soothing clicking of its blades. But the real world is not a reel world. Our lawns are big and demanding. A reel mower just can't keep up with lawns that cover more than 2,000 square feet. So we need the brute strength of a rotary mower (maybe even a riding mower) to keep them under control.

While we're mowing with that power mower, we're making the air just a little bit dirtier. Running a poorly tuned power mower for 1 hour can produce as many harmful hydrocarbons as driving a car on the highway for more than 6 hours! In fact, nearly 5 percent of all air pollution in the United States is produced by lawn and garden equipment. But if you must use a power mower, keep it in peak condition so it's running clean and doesn't have to be junked after a couple of years.

The following regular maintenance at the right time can keep your mower running right and prevent it from spewing out even more pollutants.

One-Time Maintenance. Install a wash-out port. This inexpensive, easy-to-install coupler attaches to the mower deck, allowing you to connect a hose to the mower to wash out the underside of the deck easily, without tipping the machine over.

HOW TO

Make a Flowering Low-Mow Lawn Mix

80 percent perennial ryegrass
10 percent clover
5 percent yarrow
3 percent chamomile
2 percent English daisy

Or try this simpler mix.

80 percent hard fescue
20 percent yarrow

Level, till, and rake the soil to prepare it for seeding. Sow the seed with a handheld broadcast spreader or drop-type fertilizer spreader. Rake after sowing to barely cover the seed, then firm the seeded area lightly with a roller or by tamping with the back of a rake. Sprinkle daily and mulch with weed-free straw to keep the area evenly moist until the grass is 2 inches tall.

Sharpen Your Mower Blade

A sharp mower blade cuts the grass; a dull blade tears it. The difference affects both fuel efficiency and the health and appearance of your lawn. Here's how to give your mower the edge.

1. Disconnect the spark plug wire.
2. Wedge a block of wood between the blade and the housing to keep the blade from turning.
3. Remove the bolt that holds the blade.
4. Remove the blade, and secure it in a vise.
5. Inspect the blade for dings and nicks along the cutting edge.
6. To sharpen, make even strokes with a file along the beveled edge. To ensure good balance, make an equal number of strokes on each edge of the blade.
7. Check the balance by balancing the blade on a dowel or screwdriver handle. Or use a blade balancer, available at most hardware stores for about $5.

TIPS

Know How Much It Needs

Save money (on fertilizer) and time (mowing an overfed lawn) by knowing how many pounds of actual nitrogen your lawn requires per year per 1,000 square feet.

Cool-Season Grasses

Species	Pounds of actual nitrogen required
Bentgrasses	2 to 4
Kentucky bluegrass	2 to 3
Perennial ryegrass	2 to 3
Chewings fescue	1 to 3
Hard fescue	1 to 2
Red fescue	1 to 2
Sheep fescue	1 to 2
Tall fescue	1 to 2

Warm-Season Grasses

Species	Pounds of actual nitrogen required
St. Augustinegrass	3 to 6
Bahiagrass	2 to 4
Centipedegrass	2 to 3
Zoysiagrass	2 to 3
Bermudagrass	1 to 4
Carpetgrass	1 to 3
Blue grama grass	½ to 1
Buffalograss	½ to 1

TIPS

Natural Nitrogen Sources

Once you know how much nitrogen your grass needs, you can begin shopping for fertilizer. Some garden centers offer blended organic lawn fertilizers. Check the numbers indicating the percentage of nitrogen, phosphorus and potassium (NPK). Synthetic fertilizers typically list high numbers like 10-10-10. The ideal organic fertilizer should be about 3-1-2. Or you can use traditional sources of nitrogen, such as manure or alfalfa meal.

Material	Percent nitrogen
Bloodmeal	12
Bat guano	10
Alfalfa meal	5
Fish meal	5
Poultry manure	3
Cow manure	2

In the Spring.

• Change the spark plug, setting the gap as recommended in the manual.

• Clean the engine housing. Even if your mower has been stored in a garage or shed, it may have been invaded and appropriated by mice and critters. Check inside the housing for nests, and using a screwdriver or putty knife, scrape out any debris from the housing and from the baffles or air vents. Hose out the space between the housing and the engine.

• Clean or replace the air filter if you can see dirt or grime on it. If the filter is foam, clean it with warm, soapy water. Most mower engines use paper filters that are not reusable. Replace these with new filters.

Figure Out the Fertilizer

It's not that hard to figure out how much of your chosen nitrogen source you'll need to feed your lawn adequately but without overnourishing it. To determine how much fertilizer to use per 1,000 square feet, complete the following calculations.

Pounds of actual nitrogen required per year per 1,000 square feet (from "Know How Much It Needs" on page 98)

Divided by:
Percentage of actual nitrogen in the fertilizer (from "Natural Nitrogen Sources" on page 99)

Equals:
Pounds of fertilizer required per year per 1,000 square feet

For example:
Kentucky bluegrass requires 2 pounds of actual nitrogen per year per 1,000 square feet. Bat guano fertilizer contains 10 percent (or 0.10) actual nitrogen. Two pounds (the nitrogen required) divided by 0.10 (the nitrogen provided) equals 20. So 1,000 square feet of Kentucky bluegrass would require 20 pounds of bat guano per year.

The first use of the term "lawn" in America occurred in 1733.

●Check drive belts, and replace them if they show cracks or signs of wear.

●Coat the underside of the deck with a Teflon spray to make cleanup easier.

In the Fall.

●Add fuel stabilizer. If your mower will be in storage for more than a couple of months, use a fuel stabilizer, such as Sta-Bil, to keep the gas from gumming up. That's better than draining the tank because just a drop of gas left in the line can cause problems. Add the stabilizer to gas in the tank, according to the manufacturer's instructions.

Twice a Year.

●Change the oil. Use 30-weight detergent oil, and change it every 25 mowing hours; more frequently if you have a dusty lawn. Change the oil when it's warm, and while the contaminants are suspended in the oil, rather than laying at the bottom of the engine.

Many mowers have an oil drain plug on the underside of the deck. Others can be drained through the fill plug by tipping the mower on its side.

●Sharpen the blade. A rotary mower blade needs sharpening about once a month under normal usage. You can sharpen a single blade up to 10 times before it's completely worn out.

A Greener Grass-Cutting Alternative. Conventional gasoline-powered lawn mowers are not exactly environmentally friendly. In fact, the small engines that run them spew a significant amount of nasty gasses—carbon monoxide, volatile organic compounds (VOCs), and nitrogen oxides—into the air. In 1 hour of operation, a conventional lawn mower produces as much pollution as 40 late-model cars!

What's a lawn lover to do? Go electric. They've been on the market for decades, but electric, battery-powered mowers are now improved enough to become

LAWN CARE

a sensible alternative to gas. Faster, more powerful, and able to run longer on a single charge, battery-powered mowers have a lot going for them.

New electric engines deliver up to 5 hp—enough power to cut the tallest grass easily—and can run for several hours between charges. Most new models have enough run time to cut a full ½-acre lawn and are equipped with mulching blades. They make about half as much noise as gasoline models and can be operated for under $20 worth of electricity per year. And the mowers are virtually maintenance-free. No more fiddling with the carburetor. Just sharpen the blade once a year, and go.

Look for 36-volt models with quick-charge capability. Although they take 24 hours to recharge fully, they will reach 70 percent power in just 4 hours.

Diet for a Small Plant.

When it comes to lawns, each of us is like some suburban Sisyphus, locked into an unending task. But instead of rolling a boulder uphill over and over, we're trapped in the glut-and-cut cycle of lawn care. We pour on the fertilizer, then have to race to keep the grass mowed. Besides wasting our own time and labor in this self-defeating chore, we're also wasting nitrogen, and allowing it to wash into and pollute the groundwater.

In reality, the lawn needs much less food than fertilizer companies would lead you to believe. And couldn't we all do with less time behind the mower?

To establish a proper diet for this small plant, you need only familiarize yourself with the nitrogen requirements of the grass you grow and the nitrogen content of natural fertilizers. The actual minimum amount of nitrogen required varies from species to species (as shown in the chart on page 98), but it can be as little as 1 pound of nitrogen per 1,000 square feet per year.

A Natural Advantage. For starters, don't even buy fertilizer: Just leave the clippings on the lawn when you mow. This provides your turf up to 2 pounds of nitrogen per year. After that, go for the compost—apply about half an inch every year, using a drop spreader. Both these practices will cut down substantially on the amount of fertilizer you need to buy for your lawn. And before you add a single crumb of fertilizer to your lawn, get your soil tested to see if there are any imbalances that might interfere with your lawn's health.

Whipping Weeds.

Weeds in the lawn? Now that's a fly in the ointment. The lawn, by conventional definition, is a monocrop, consisting of grass plants and nothing but grass plants—as many as 850 per square foot, 3 million per acre, 150 trillion blanketing the United States.

So Americans spend billions of dollars per year dousing the lawn with dangerous herbicides—some even suspected carcinogens—all to make the front yard resemble a golf green. That time could be better spent ridding our minds of unrealistic expectations.

Studies have shown that a lawn with up to 20 percent "weeds" is just as pleasing to the eye as a 100 percent weed-free lawn. Weeds that exceed that level can be dealt with without dangerous chemicals.

Use a Natural Herbicide. In the mid-1980s, researchers at Iowa State University accidentally discovered that corn gluten meal—the stuff that's used as filler in pet and livestock food—is a highly effective natural turf herbicide. It works as a preemergent to kill plantain, creeping bentgrass, dandelion, and

Among male "home enthusiasts," yard work is a more popular activity than sex.

many other weeds. Apply 10–20 pounds per 1,000 square feet in spring before weeds begin to sprout.

Weed 'Em. What would you do if you found weeds in your vegetable garden or flowerbed? Would you douse them with herbicide? No, you'd yank them out. Long-handled, specialty weeding tools for the lawn, such as the Hound Dog Weeder and the Speedy Weedy, make a surprisingly fast and easy job of pulling dandelions, plantain, and other lawn weeds.

Mow 'Em. Studies have shown that you can reduce crabgrass by as much as 40 percent over 5 years just by raising the height of the mower deck from 1¼ to 2¼ inches. Mowing high invigorates the grass so it outcompetes weeds and shades the soil to deter the germination of weed seeds.

Scorch 'Em. Finally, for the backyard Rambo, here's one of the most exciting ways to get rid of weeds. Borrowing a trick from organic agriculture, gardeners can buy a weed torch, something like a long-handled blowtorch, to fry the weeds. Take careful aim—those flames will scorch grass, too. Don't use it during drought, and always have water or fire-extinguishing equipment handy when you set out to sear a few weeds.

Conformity is the rule in the suburbs. There are standards for the appearance of our house and yard. Keep the house painted, keep the lawn mowed. But do we all have to have the same rather uninteresting shrubs lined up in front of the house?

Foundation's Triumph. Foundation planting was born in the '50s as a means of disguising the concrete foundations of ranch houses. Unfortunately, it's still stuck in the past. The foundation area is a vast suburban wasteland, but it doesn't have to be that way. You won't be expelled from the neighborhood if you try something more creative. On the contrary, your neighbors will probably thank you—or at least follow your lead.

Test the Limits. Break out of the boring foundation-planting box. Incorporate a theme. Use the foundation area as a place to experiment with plants that might not otherwise survive in your region. Take advantage of the microclimate. Snug up against the house, the foundation area is likely to be significantly warmer than the rest of your landscape, making it a great place to try plants that normally grow farther south.

Choose plants that don't require a lot of maintenance. That means perennials that don't need a lot of water and plants that can stand the heat. Shade is an important consideration, too—take note of where shadows fall throughout the day and choose plants accordingly. Use slow-growing plants that won't need lots of pruning to keep them from outgrowing their space.

Take advantage of the structure. Screw some eye-bolts into the side of the house just above the foundation and just below the eaves, and string 9-gauge wire between them to make an easy trellis for climbing plants such as clematis or morning glory.

In short, use the area immediately outside your front door (and all around your house) to create plantings that please you. Don't fall prey to the cookie-cutter look that's ruled the suburbs for too long. And, if your house came with the standard-issue skirting of drab yews, rhododendrons, and/or arborvitae, it's never too late to reclaim that space. Spruce them up with long-blooming perennials and flowering shrubs, or simply rip 'em out and start fresh.

Foundation Food. Put your foundation to work with fruit trees and vegetable plants. Try blueberry bushes, dwarf apple trees, lettuce and other greens, or even a well-behaved tomato plant or two. Or make over your

All the cut flowers in a vase of water will last longer if the arrangement includes foxgloves.

FOUNDATIONS, FLOWERS, AND MORE

FOUNDATIONS, FLOWERS, AND MORE

foundation area into a classy herb bed. Imagine the pleasure of stepping out the door to pluck fruits, herbs, or vegetables for your next meal. It sure beats stepping out the door to prune back the yew that's growing over your picture window!

Foundation Natives. There's no better place to make a statement about your love of native plants than the front of the house. Check with local nurseries, your county's Cooperative Extension office, or regional gardening books for the best native plants for your area and growing conditions. Here are a few shrubs, small trees, grasses, and perennials to get you started.

In the Northeast.
- Eastern redbud (*Cercis canadensis*)
- Northern sea oats (*Chasmanthium latifolium*)
- Black huckleberry (*Gaylussacia baccata*)
- Mountain laurel (*Kalmia latifolia*)
- Cinnamon fern (*Osmunda cinnamomea*)

In the Southeast.
- Carolina allspice or common sweetshrub (*Calycanthus floridus*)
- Virginia sweetspire (*Itea virginica*)
- Southern magnolia (*Magnolia grandiflora*)
- Dwarf palmetto (*Sabal minor*)

In the Midwest.
- Saskatoon serviceberry (*Amelanchier alnifolia*)
- Smooth aster (*Aster laevis*)
- Joe-Pye weed (*Eupatorium purpureum*)
- Prairie gentian (*Eustoma grandiflorum*)
- Arkansas rose (*Rosa arkansana*)

In the Northwest.
- Salal (*Gaultheria shallon*)
- Licorice fern (*Polypodium hesperium*)
- Pacific rhododendron (*Rhododendron macrophyllum*)
- False hellebore (*Veratrum viride*)

In the Southwest.
- Bigberry manzanita (*Arctostaphylos glauca*)
- California lilacs (*Ceanothus* spp.)
- California poppies (*Eschscholzia californica*)
- California fuchsia (*Zauschneria californica*)

Foundation Fun. Do something different—just for fun. Plant a collection of cacti. Fill the area with ornamental grasses. Or give the front of the house a tropical look—even in the North. Move your houseplants out for the summer. Buy exotics and use them as annuals in front of the house. Give the neighbors something to talk about.

Taking Shrubberies Seriously. "We
want you to bring us some shrubberies," demanded Monty Python's knights who said "Ni." And they were on the right track. Better known as shrubs here in the United States, these plants are too often overlooked in the landscape.

Build the Soil First

Take the time to thoroughly prepare the soil for your foundation planting. Often the foundation area contains mostly subsoil that has been backfilled up against the house. Work in plenty of organic matter or compost to give your plants a fighting chance.

Be a Savvy Plant Shopper

Is a plant in a pot like a pig in a poke? And how about a plant all trussed up in twine and burlap? How can you tell if the plant you're paying for is a good buy and a healthy specimen?

Before you shell out your hard-earned bucks on some pretty perennial or supposedly stalwart shrub, inspect each plant thoroughly to make sure it's worth taking home to your garden.

Take a Look at the Top.

First, look at the obvious: the trunk/stem and branches. Don't buy any plants that show nicks or cuts in the bark. Be wary of plants with crowded masses of thin and weak branches and any with black-tipped branches or wilted or discolored leaves.

Get to the Root of the Matter.

Then take a look at the roots. That's easy with potted plants. Carefully remove the plant from the container or, better yet, have a nursery employee do it for you.

The roots should be light-colored, fibrous, and thick enough to hold the soil in place. If you see more soil than roots, or if the soil falls away from the roots, reject that plant. It's probably a bareroot plant that was recently transplanted into the container. Its lack of roots will give it a slow start in the garden, and it may require extra care. Large brown roots wrapped around each other mean the plant is rootbound. That's not necessarily a deal-killer, but a rootbound plant will lack vigor unless and until you do some serious root pruning.

Checking the roots of a balled-and-burlapped plant is a bit trickier. Rather than unwrap the whole thing and risk getting tossed from the nursery, look for damage to the burlap. If the wrapping is ripped, the roots inside may be injured as well. Squeeze the rootball. You should be able to feel a firm root mass inside. If the burlap feels soft and empty, it may contain a bareroot plant that was recently packaged in a soil ball. Such a plant may not have enough healthy roots to withstand transplanting into your garden.

Say shrubs, and most folks think of ubiquitous green meatballs that flank front doors from Maine to Mississippi. By sheer numbers, they've eclipsed a world of more interesting plants.

It's a shame that other shrubs have gotten short shrift. Longer-lasting than perennials, more constant than annuals, shrubs pack a lot of power. It takes only a few to transform a landscape—as a dramatic backdrop to a sitting area, in a hedge for privacy, or as a feature of a naturalistic planting. With blooms, berries, and colorful foliage, shrubs can offer year-round landscape interest in virtually any part of the country. Just a few well-placed and well-chosen shrubs can provide almost continuous color, from the bright yellow blooms of witch hazel in late winter to the fiery fall foliage of its cousin *Disanthus*.

Tree Planting Myths Felled. When it

comes to planting trees, everything you've been told is wrong. Or at least, everything that seems to make sense, doesn't. When we plant trees and shrubs, we have to fight the urge to baby them. You might think that the best thing you can do when planting

(continued on page 112)

Shrubs That Work

Shrubs don't have to be boring! Forget what you know about how shrubs are *supposed* to look, and try some of the plants listed below to brighten up your landscape without endless hours of planting annuals or tending perennials.

FOR SPRING COLOR

Name	Height	Hardiness	Comments
Buttercup winterhazel (*Corylopsis pauciflora*)	4 to 6 feet	Zones 6 to 9	Yellow blossoms in early spring; good-looking foliage through summer
Beautybush (*Kolkwitzia amabilis*)	6 to 10 feet	Zones 5 to 9	Delicate pink flowers with yellow markings; attractive bark
Sargent crab apple (*Malus sargenntii*)	6 to 8 feet	Zones 4 to 8	Very fragrant white flowers in spring; tiny red fruit in fall
Spirea (*Spiraea thunbergii* 'Ogon')	2 to 4 feet	Zones 3 to 8	Clusters of small, but early, white flowers; light green foliage
Manchurian lilac (*Syringa pubescens* subsp. *patula* 'Miss Kim')	6 to 8 feet	Zones 4 to 8	Short, mildew-resistant lilac with fragrant purple flowers in late spring
Chinese snowball viburnum (*Viburnum macrocephalum*)	15 to 20 feet	Zones 7 to 9	Gigantic balls of flowers that fade from chartreuse to white

FOR SUMMER COLOR

Name	Height	Hardiness	Comments
'Edward Goucher' glossy abelia (*Abelia* × 'Edward Goucher')	5 feet	Zones 6 to 9	Purplish pink flowers last until frost, when leaves turn bronze and purple
Bottlebrush buckeye (*Aesculus parviflora*)	8 to 12 feet	Zones 5 to 9	Pure white flowers in summer; bright yellow fall foliage
'Hummingbird' sweet pepperbush (*Clethra alnifolia* 'Hummingbird')	3 to 4 feet	Zones 3 to 9	Fragrant white flowers on an attractive, mounding plant
Oakleaf hydrangea (*Hydrangea quercifolia*)	4 to 6 feet	Zones 5 to 9	White flowers; good fall color; handsome russet, orange, and red bark
Golden St. John's wort (*Hypericum frondosum* 'Sunburst')	3 to 4 feet	Zones 5 to 8	Yellow flowers in summer; blue-green foliage
'Henry's Garnet' sweetspire (*Itea virginica* 'Henry's Garnet')	3 to 5 feet	Zones 5 to 9	Grows in any soil or light; white flowers; red fall foliage

FOR FALL COLOR

Name	Height	Hardiness	Comments
'Autumn Brilliance' serviceberry (*Amelanchier × grandiflora* 'Autumn Brilliance')	15 to 25 feet	Zones 4 to 9	Large white, late-blooming flowers; vibrant red fall color
Chokeberry (*Aronia arbutifolia*)	6 to 8 feet	Zones 5 to 9	Colorful fall foliage; red berries
Disanthus (*Disanthus cercidifolius*)	6 to 10 feet	Zones 5 to 8	Handsome red, purple, and orange fall foliage
Fothergilla (*Fothergilla major*)	6 to 10 feet	Zones 5 to 8	Fragrant white bottlebrush flowers in spring; fall foliage is bright yellow and orange
PeeGee hydrangea (*Hydrangea paniculata*)	10 to 20 feet	Zones 4 to 8	Late-summer clusters of creamy white flowers fade to bronze in fall through winter
'Erie' linden viburnum (*Viburnum dilatatum* 'Erie')	6 to 9 feet	Zones 5 to 8	Red fruits appear at end of summer and turn coral-pink with first frost

FOR WINTER COLOR

Name	Height	Hardiness	Comments
Chinese witchhazel (*Hamamelis mollis*)	10 to 15 feet	Zones 5 to 9	Usually the first shrub to bloom in late winter, producing fragrant flowers in January, February, or March
'Sparkleberry' holly (*Ilex* 'Sparkleberry')	18 feet	Zones 5 to 9	This deciduous holly produces long-lasting, bright red fruits on bare stems
Winterberry (*Ilex verticillata*)	8 to 10 feet	Zones 5 to 8	Native holly with colorful berries that last into winter; 'Nana' has especially large berries
Bayberry (*Myrica pensylvanica*)	To 9 feet	Zones 3 to 6	Evergreen-scented leaves remain on the shrub until early winter; small waxy fruit
Heavenly bamboo (*Nandina domestica*)	To 8 feet	Zones 6 to 9	Evergreen shrub with graceful leaves that turn maroon in autumn; red berries last through winter
American elder (*Sambucus canadensis*)	To 12 feet	Zones 4 to 9	Clusters of white flowers in spring and summer; small berries attract birds throughout winter

a tree or shrub is to mix copious quantities of peat, compost, manure, or any other rich soil amendments into the planting hole. Wrong. As strange as it may seem, that's about the worst thing you can do. In fact, that sort of obsessive planting hole supplementation leads to the dreaded "flowerpot effect." That is, if the soil in the planting hole is rich and loose and the surrounding soil is not, the roots will stay put and won't venture into the surrounding soil.

HOW TO

Tepees to Save Space Elegantly

Short on space but longing to grow a good selection of heirloom tomatoes? Build a good-looking bamboo tepee and grow four vigorous plants in 4 square feet of garden space. To make tomato tepees, you'll need bamboo stakes and sturdy string.

Four 7-foot bamboo stakes
3-foot length of twine or leather shoelace

Lash the tops of the four stakes together, and space the other ends of the poles 4 feet apart. Plant a tomato at the base of each pole, and prune each to two stems, tying the stems to the bamboo poles as the plants grow. Bamboo tepees also are ideal for growing pole beans, scarlet runner beans, or morning glories.

Maybe the plant will flourish in that luxurious atmosphere for the first year or two, but after that it will languish. Digging it up years later (or picking it up because it's blown over), you'd find that the roots are still right there in that plush planting hole, circling around each other as though they were in a flowerpot. To avoid the pitfalls of poorly planted trees and the expense of replacing them, follow these steps for tree (and shrub) planting success.

1. Dig a wide, shallow hole. The planting hole should be no deeper than the rootball or container and two or three times as wide. Rather than amending the soil, puncture the sides and bottom of the hole with a pitchfork to allow the roots easier entry into the surrounding soil.

2. When you're ready to plant, fill the planting hole about one-half full of water and let it drain.

3. If the plant is potted, remove it from the pot and check to see if it's rootbound. If the roots are wrapped around each other, gently loosen them. For balled-and-burlapped plants, strip off as much of the burlap as possible without damaging the roots. If the roots are winding around each other, gently pry them loose.

4. Stick the plant in the hole at a depth that's the same or just slightly higher (to allow for settling) than its depth in the container or soil ball. Refill with the native soil, tamping it in place. Soak the soil with water, then cover with a 2-inch-deep layer of mulch, making sure that the mulch does not touch the trunk.

5. For large trees and in high-wind areas, carefully wrap a padded rope around the trunk, and stake the tree in place to keep it from rocking itself loose in the planting hole. Remove the stakes and wires after no more than 1 year.

Nationwide, only 1 percent of all tallgrass prairie remains intact.

Make a Mini-Meadow.
As landscape solutions, meadows and prairies sound too good to be true: Sow a bunch of wildflower seeds, let them grow, mow or burn once a year, and sit back and enjoy the wildlife. Forget about constant mowing, watering, and chemical applications. But if you try that laissez-faire approach, what you wind up with is something resembling less a luxurious, colorful meadow and more a weedy, abandoned lot.

It's true that once established, a meadow or prairie requires less work and less input than a lawn or flowerbed, but not without proper preparation.

It's best to start small. Rather than remaking your entire yard, start with a 100- to 200-square-foot strip at the edge of your property or along a sidewalk or driveway. Design the mini-meadow to incorporate soft curves rather than squares or sharp angles. And don't rely on seeds alone. Combine them with transplants of natives and wildflowers to get things off to a quicker start.

There are two simple ways to start the planting.

Starting from Scratch.

- Dig the area as thoroughly as if you were planting a vegetable garden or perennial bed, removing as many roots, stolons, and tubers as possible. The easiest way to remove sod is with a sod-stripper, available from most tool rental shops.
- Sow a low-maintenance bunch grass, such as hard fescue in the North or buffalograss in the South, at one-half the recommended rate.
- Mark off planting areas at random spots, 2 to 3 feet apart, and plant transplants or sow wildflower seed in those spots. Keep those areas grass- and weed-free until the plants germinate.

Planting in Patches.

If you're replacing turf with wildflowers, you can let the existing grass do the weed-smothering work for you. Instead of removing all of the turf, just strip patches and pockets of it. Plant those areas with wildflower plants or seeds, and gradually remove more and more of the lawn from year to year. For best results, install a temporary edging around the plant pockets to keep the grass from invading.

Go Wild with These Plants.

To make a mini-meadow or pocket prairie, choose plants that are easy to grow, have long bloom periods, spread vigorously, and are native—or at least well adapted to—your area. Below are a few ideas to get you started. Check with local nurseries, your local Co-operative Extension office, or your state's Department of Natural Resources to learn more about the selection of native or adapted plants that are recommended for your area.

Meadow Plants for the East and Midwest.

- Butterfly weed (*Asclepias tuberosa*)
- Purple coneflower (*Echinacea purpurea*)
- Queen of the prairie (*Filipendula rubra*)
- Meadowsweet (*Filipendula ulmaria*)
- Eulalia grass (*Miscanthus sinensis*)
- Bee balm (*Monarda didyma*)
- Moss phlox (*Phlox subulata*)

Prairie Plants for the Plains and Far West (Moist Soil).

- Prairie coreopsis (*Coreopsis palmata*)
- Pale purple coneflower (*Echinacea pallida*)
- Boneset (*Eupatorium perfoliatum*)
- Pale spiked lobelia (*Lobelia spicata*)
- Wild bergamot (*Monarda fistulosa*)

Prairie Plants for the Plains and Far West (Dry Soil).

- Big bluestem grass (*Andropogon gerardii*)
- Flowering spurge (*Euphorbia corollata*)
- Prairie smoke (*Geum triflorum*)
- Prairie cinquefoil (*Potentilla arguta*)
- Prairie dropseed (*Sporobolus heterolepsis*)

Sod-Busting without Roundup.

Whether you're planting a mini-meadow, a pocket prairie, or a traditional flowerbed or vegetable garden, if you're starting fresh, you need to clear a spot to work in. Too often, when faced with weeds or grass to clear, gardeners automatically reach for the Roundup. In a few short years, this broad-spectrum, nonselective herbicide, made with glyphosate, has become the weed killer of choice. In fact, it's estimated that for 1998, over 112,000 metric tons of the stuff was used worldwide. And 71 percent of genetically engineered crops planted

in 1998 are designed to be resistant to herbicide—mainly Roundup.

Why is glyphosate so popular? It works pretty well in wiping out weeds. And it has been touted as safe. But it may not be as safe as gardeners have been led to believe. First, it was discovered that glyphosate was disrupting the beneficial microbial life in the soil. And now, there's more seriously scary news. A recent study by Swedish researchers shows a link between

Swedish sufferers of non-Hodgkins

HOW TO

Make a Window-Frame Trellis

For the cozy cottage garden look, you can turn the side of your house, garage, or garden shed into a trellis.

4 screw eyes
9-gauge wire
4 turnbuckles
4 stakes

Fasten a screw eye at each corner of a window. Attach a turnbuckle and a length of wire to each eye. Stretch the wires from the top corners down the sides of the window to the bottom corners; stretch wire from the two bottom corners to stakes in the ground. Tighten the turnbuckles to pull the wires taut. Sow pole beans, runner beans, morning glories, or other annual flowering vines at each stake.

lymphoma were 2.3 times more likely to have had contact with the herbicide glyphosate.

glyphosate and non-Hodgkins lymphoma. Folks with that cancer were more than twice as likely to have handled glyphosate than those without the cancer.

What's the alternative to this alleged weed cure-all? There are several physical and cultural ways to eliminate weeds naturally and safely.

Mulch 'Em. This is the easiest, although not the fastest or the most aesthetically pleasing way to rid a large patch of ground of weeds or to bust sod to plant a garden. Simply cover the ground with a black plastic mulch (preferably 2 mil or thicker), cardboard, or any other opaque material. Leave the mulch in place for 2 to 4 months, depending on your climate and the time of year. (In the North, it makes sense to cover the ground in autumn and remove the mulch in spring.) Remove the mulch, and the turf and its roots will be much decomposed, leaving the soil weed-free, fluffy, and probably teeming with earthworms. If you don't like the idea of staring at a patch of plastic mulch for months, cover it with shredded leaves or grass clippings for a slightly better look.

Solarize 'Em. This method uses a clear plastic mulch to fry weed seeds. Work the soil first, removing as many existing weeds as possible. Then, water the area well and cover with a sheet of 2-mil-thick clear plastic, making sure the sides are fastened securely at soil level. Leave the plastic in place for at least 6 to 8 weeks in summer, depending on the climate— the hotter the weather, the less time required.

Burn 'Em. The most ancient of all methods of clearing brush has gone high-tech. Now you can buy a weed-blasting propane torch from garden supply stores to fry existing weeds and sterilize weed seeds.

It's not necessary to scorch the weed to a crisp—just hold the flame about 3 inches above the plant for a few seconds and the heat will cause it to dehydrate and die. Just make sure to have a water source handy in case flames threaten to get out of control. Flaming your weeds away works best in the spring, when the plants are young and tender.

Strip 'Em. Rent a sod-stripper from your local tool rental shop. This gasoline-powered machine will make quick work of peeling the sod from a lawn. Add the sod strips to the compost pile, and rake the bare ground thoroughly to remove weed roots.

Till 'Em. Tillers weren't made for chopping up existing lawns. Removing turf with a tiller is a tough and tiring job that requires several passes to eliminate the turf. There are easier ways to do it. But the rotary tiller is still a good way to break garden soil in the spring and to eliminate weeds from gardens and large expanses of tilled soil.

Growing Up the Right Way. Trellising is another way to add pizzazz to your landscape without a lot of fuss. Growing vining plants upward over a structure provides vertical interest in your yard in a much shorter time than growing a tree or shrub to its mature height. The key is finding a trellis you like that's durable, strong, attractive, easy to set up and take down, and made from inexpensive, readily available material.

Here are a few suggestions for building sturdy, long-lasting trellises: aluminum electrical conduit (connect with elbows and tees), PVC or copper pipe, chain-link fencing, or wood lattice.

GROWING YOUR OWN VEGETABLES AND FRUIT

About 20,000,000 bales of Canadian peat, weighing 750,000 metric tonnes,

All winter, you read about the latest and greatest varieties of vegetables and flowers, only to find that the local nurseries aren't growing them. Often the only way to get organic seedlings of a new variety—or an heirloom—is to grow them from seeds.

Sow and Grow. To the neophyte, seed starting seems like a messy, complicated, expensive, time-consuming process. It doesn't necessarily have to be. You just need to provide the essentials: light, heat, and water in sufficient quantities.

Light: Think 16. That's 16 hours a day, 2 to 3 inches away from the plants. That seems like a lot of light, but that's what seedlings need. They won't get that much on a windowsill, but a fluorescent shop light fixture will do just fine. You don't need special grow bulbs; regular fluorescent tubes provide enough light and cost much less. Use a timer to make sure they go on and off as needed. Hang the shop lights with a chain for easy raising and lowering, or use clothesline and a pulley to maintain the 2- to 3-inch distance as your seedlings grow.

Soil: Dirt Won't Do. Regular old garden soil is too heavy for seed starting. So is normal potting soil. Seedlings need a light, porous mix that drains quickly to prevent disease. The optimal material for this is peat, and that's why seed-starting mixes are primarily peat. Even though peat is a renewable natural resource, the rate of renewal is very slow. While the Canadian peat industry maintains that peat is being renewed faster than it's being harvested, you may wish to use a peat-free seed-starting mix.

Unfortunately, peat-free mixes can be hard to find. If you choose to make your own seed-starting mix, you can reduce the amount of peat you use by replacing up to one-third of the peat with screened, mature compost. As an added bonus, the compost will gently fertilize your seedlings and help fend off the fungi that cause damping-off disease.

Purchase Peat-Free

Many garden centers and mail-order sources stock peat alternatives for seed starting. Try coconut fiber (coir) or bagasse (a by-product of sugarcane processing). If you go the route of peat-perlite/vermiculite seed-starting mixes, go for the organic brand: Many ready-made mixes also contain chemical fertilizers.

are harvested and sold annually.

GROWING YOUR OWN VEGETABLES AND FRUIT

Water: Soak and Wait. Once the seedlings emerge, don't just spritz or mist the plants. It's the soil you want to water, not the plants. Make sure it's thoroughly wet, top to bottom, then let it dry out thoroughly before watering again. Ideally, water your seedlings from the bottom up by placing their pots or flats in a tray of water and letting it soak upward, then removing any standing water once the soil is wet clear through.

Fertilizer: Feed Lightly. Overfed plants get tall and leggy before their time. Feed seedlings lightly with fish emulsion or liquid seaweed. If you've mixed compost into your seed-starting mix, you'll probably need very little supplemental fertilizer, if any.

TIPS

Peat-Free "Potty" Pots

Peat pots are hard to beat for utility and cost when starting lots of seeds. If you like the convenience of peat pots when starting seeds but don't like the idea of using peat, try a peat-free, totally free, recycled alternative. Just collect cardboard toilet paper tubes, and line them up side by side in a flat. Fill with seed-starting soil mix, and sow. These "potty" pots are tall enough to provide extra room for the growing roots of large plants like tomatoes and squash. When your seedlings are ready to move into your garden, plant them, "pots" and all.

Temperature: From the Bottom Up. Nothing speeds seed germination as much as bottom heat. Use a horticultural heating cable or a waterproof heating pad to provide bottom heat until the seedlings appear. You can keep heat-lovers like tomatoes and peppers on the heat mat until you're ready to move them into your garden. Shut off the heat under cool-weather crops such as broccoli and cabbage once the seedlings are up and growing.

Fruit Trees: The Kindest Cut.

Just the thought of pruning alone is enough to frighten many otherwise capable people out of growing their own fruits. In fact, pruning a fruit tree may be the most intimidating act in all of gardening. What could be more scary that standing face to face with an innocent shrub or tree while equipped with a sharp pair of pruning shears in your hand and just a little bit of knowledge in your head? Relax. For the most part, it's difficult to do major damage to a tree simply by pruning it.

Pruning Basics. Although some tree species have their own specific pruning requirements, there are some basic commonsense rules that you can apply to almost all of them.

As a rule of thumb, pruning is best done during a tree's winter dormancy, usually in late winter to early spring before the buds swell and open (also referred to as "bud break"). A light summer pruning, just after the major flush of spring growth, helps increase fruit production.

Most people know they're supposed to prune fruit trees, but not everyone understands why. Here are explanations of the three most common types of pruning cuts made on fruit trees.

• To increase vigor: Remove suckers and water-sprouts. Watersprouts are the young spindly growths that grow vertically from the base of the plant. Suckers are the thin, young growths that emerge from branches. Remove them all. They're worthless, and they sap strength from the tree.

• To admit light and air: Cut out top branches that shade the lower part of the tree and thin out bottom branches that are crowding each other.

• To remove crossed branches: As crossed branches rub against each other, they damage the bark and create entry points for disease and insects. Also, eliminate branches that form sharp crotch angles. Sharply angled branches are subject to breakage. Furthermore, most lead to vertical branches, while horizontal ones bear more fruit.

TIPS

Hold the Dressing

Years ago, gardeners were told to make cuts flush with branches and slather with wound dressing. Now we're told both suggestions were wrong. Instead, leave a "branch collar," a 1- to 2-inch-long stub, when removing a branch. Don't use a wound dressing, also sold as pruning paint, as such products impair the natural healing process.

No matter how much money you spend on plants or how much you baby them, they're not going to thrive unless the soil that supports them is in decent shape. Without good soil, your plants will never look as good or produce as much as they should.

The Soil's the Secret. It's a bit of a cliché, but soil is the foundation that supports your garden. If that foundation's weak, there's not much hope for a successful garden. But you can't fix it until you know what's broke. So first you need to check the condition, texture, pH, and fertility of your soil.

Type and Texture. Your soil texture will tell you a lot about how much and how often to water and feed your garden. Sandy soils, for example, need much more water, while clay soils are generally the highest in fertility. Most fertilizer recommendations vary according to the makeup of the soil.

With a quart jar and some water, you can conduct a simple yet fairly accurate test to find out what kind of particles dominate in your soil and, therefore, what its texture is.

1. Collect about a half-quart of soil from several locations in your garden or lawn.

2. Let the soil dry, then fill a quart glass jar about two-thirds full of water mixed with 1 teaspoon of dishwashing liquid. Slowly pour in the soil until the jar is full. Put on the lid and shake the jar for 1 minute, then set it on a level surface.

3. Let the soil settle for 2 days. As it does, it will separate into three layers, with sand (the largest particles) on the bottom, silt in the middle, and clay (the smallest particles) on top. By comparing the size of each layer, you can determine the relative proportions of each particle type in your soil. If any one layer makes up more than half of the soil, your soil is classified as that type.

Clay garden soil typically contains about 60 percent clay, 30 percent silt, and 10 percent sand. *Loam* soils are about 20 percent clay, 40 percent silt, and 40 percent sand. *Sandy* loam is 10 percent clay, 20 percent silt, and 70 percent sand.

If your soil is more than 60 percent clay or 70 percent sand, dig in a 2-inch layer of compost to make it more workable and to improve its fertility.

Test for Fertility. You can buy a soil test kit to do it yourself, but it's worth the effort and expense to send your soil out to a lab for nutrient testing.

About 1.7 billion tons of American topsoil are lost to erosion each year.

BUILDING SOIL AND COOKING COMPOST

BUILDING SOIL AND COOKING COMPOST

Ideally, you'll use a lab that will test for organic matter content, too, and that will offer recommendations in terms of organic fertilizers.

First, call the lab, whether it's your county's cooperative extension office or a private testing agency, and ask for a collection kit. To prepare a sample for soil testing, dig soil from 4 to 8 inches deep in several spots in your garden. Make sure to use a clean trowel or other tool. Mix the soil samples together and send them off to the lab in the package provided. Test as early as possible in the spring to allow time to add nutrients before the growing season.

Test for pH. The letters pH stand for potential hydrogen, and they represent a measure (on a scale of 0 to 14) of the soil's relative acidity or alkalinity. Neutral is 7.0, anything below that is acidic, and anything over 7.0 is alkaline. Why is pH important? If the soil is too acidic or too alkaline, nutrients may

Low-Tech Soil Test

In spring, while the soil is moist and warm (at least 55°F), find an area of the garden where the ground is covered by mulch or growing plants, and dig up a chunk 1 foot square x 6 inches deep. Place the soil on a piece of wood or cardboard, and count the earthworms in the mass of soil. If you find 10 or more earthworms, your soil has good fertility.

HOW TO

Ribbon Test for Texture

Easier and faster—but not as precise as the jar test—is the ribbon test. Mix together a handful of soil, then moisten it thoroughly. Now, roll it between your palms to form a dirt rope. If it holds together and feels sticky, it's mostly clay. If it feels smooth and silky and holds together for a little bit, then it's silt. If it feels gritty and breaks apart immediately, it's mostly sand.

be bound up and not available to your plants. For most general gardening purposes, a pH of 6.0 to 7.0 is ideal. (Take a soil test to determine your soil pH.) Adding a ½- to 1-inch layer of compost is an excellent way to moderate the pH of mildly acidic or alkaline soils. In more severe cases, you can use lime to raise the pH of acidic soil or sulfur to lower the pH of alkaline soil, according to the recommendations on your soil test.

To raise soil pH 1 point, from 5.5 to 6.5, requires different amounts of lime, depending on soil type. In sandy soil, a 1-point pH change takes 30 pounds of lime per 1,000 square feet. For clay soil, you'll need to add 110 pounds of lime to make the same change. To lower the pH from 7.5 to 6.5, add 10 pounds of sulfur per 1,000 square feet to sandy soil and 20 pounds of sulfur for clay soil.

HOW TO

Rabbit manure has the highest nitrogen content of all manures—up to 2.5 percent.

The Art of Compost. Actual composting requires a little effort and science. Making compost involves more than piling stuff in a heap, but it's not brain surgery, either. In fact, no matter what you do, *you're* not making compost. The organisms that inhabit the heap are the ones who are doing the work. All you have to do is to provide a balanced diet and favorable conditions for the organisms—from bacteria and fungi to earthworms and spiders—that convert organic matter into nutrient-available compost. The better you feed them, the faster they work, and the more efficiently they release nitrogen, phosphorus, potassium, and other nutrients that your plants need.

The more active a role you play in the composting process, the faster you'll get finished compost. And the faster the compost production process, the higher the nutrient value of the finished material. You can just throw stuff in a heap in the back corner of your lot and forget about it. In a year or two, it will have decomposed to humus—terrific stuff for improving soil tilth. Or you can manage the process by containing the material, and turning and watering the compost until it's done. When it is done, the fast-track compost will be higher in nutrients than that heap that you left to its own devices.

Bin There. You don't absolutely need a bin to contain your microscopic menagerie, but it helps. A structure will keep the material in place, keep the compost from drying out, and allow easy turning. Your bin doesn't have to be expensive or even pretty; it just needs to be big enough (at least 3 feet tall by 3 feet wide) to hold all the stuff. It has to allow airflow and easy access for turning the compost. Many people use pallets nailed or wired together. Another good choice is a simple wire cylinder.

Dung That. In the eyes of decomposing organisms, there are only two basic types of raw material in the universe: carbon material and nitrogen material. You can't make compost without both of them, and they have to be in approximately the right propositions to satisfy the heap-dwelling organisms.

Whip Up a Batch of Basic Compost

1. Start with 3 parts carbon material—that's dry, brown stuff—such as straw, dried garden refuse, leaves, shredded bark, etc.

2. Add 1 part nitrogen material—that's moist, green stuff—such as grass clippings, fresh garden refuse, food scraps, etc.

3. Pile them in alternating layers 3 to 6 inches deep, until the pile is at least 3 feet high. Toss in a shovelful of soil or compost between each layer to introduce the microorganisms that will turn your debris into compost. Water, keeping the ingredients about as damp as a squeezed-out sponge.

4. The most active decomposing critters will eventually congregate in the warm and moist middle of the pile. Turn the material once or twice during the first few months to mix thoroughly, and to redistribute the organisms throughout. When adding new material, dig it into the middle of the heap. The compost is "cooked" and ready to use when it's dark brown and crumbly and smells like freshly turned soil.

TENDING
YOUR
TOOLS

One of the great pleasures of gardening comes from working with quality tools. But in order for a tool to continue working well, it requires regular cleaning and sharpening, and perhaps even an occasional reconditioning or repair.

Tools for Tools. It's never convenient when a tool breaks or wears out or otherwise fails, and it always seems to happen when you're right in the middle of a task. Make sure you're ready when the blade dulls or the handle snaps by equipping your tool shed with all the equipment you need for maintenance and repair of garden tools.

Tool First-Aid Kit. Here's a list of the tools and materials to have on hand when you need to repair or refurbish your favorite shovel, your best hoe, or some other irreplaceable garden tool.

- Wire brush for cleaning dirt, rust, and grime from blades of hand tools
- Portable drill with wire wheel, sander wheel, and buffer wheel for sharpening and polishing
- Mill bastard file for rough sharpening
- Fine-grit diamond file for fine sharpening
- Synthetic grease to lubricate moving parts
- Mineral oil to protect bare metals
- Linseed oil to preserve handles
- Pliers, screwdriver, and hole punch for extricating bolts, handles, etc.
- Vise and clamps to hold tools for repairs
- Safety goggles or other protective eyewear to use when filing, sanding, brushing, or buffing

Getting a Handle on Tools. Sooner or later, a handle snaps on your favorite hoe or shovel. All right, so the handles don't exactly snap all by themselves. Maybe we left the hoe out in the garden and lost it under a wave of luxuriant weeds, where it had to endure rain, sleet, and snow until decay played its natural role. Or perhaps we used the shovel to try to pry a boulder out of a garden bed. Instead of tossing that tool in the trash and running to the hardware store to replace the entire tool, it makes more sense to save the business end and rejuvenate the tool by attaching a new handle. It saves money (you can buy a replacement handle for half the cost of a full tool). It saves material. And it's not that difficult.

Steel is America's most recycled material—over 100 billion pounds per year.

TENDING YOUR TOOLS

First, find the correct replacement handle. Bring what's left of the tool to the local hardware store to find a suitable size replacement. Or shop through the mail or online. Mail-order garden tool companies, such as A. M. Leonard, offer a good selection of replacement handles.

Back home, secure the blade of the tool in a vise to remove the remnants of the handle.

Pry the broken handle out from the hasp. If the handle is attached by a rivet through the hasp, grind or file the head from the rivet and drive the pin through using a punch and hammer.

Pull the handle from the hasp. If the handle is jammed into the hasp, use an electric drill to split it into pieces, and then remove it. For a shovel, use a short length of rebar and a hammer to drive the handle out from the bottom of the hasp.

Before attaching a new handle, clean and sharpen the blade. Use a wire brush on a hand drill to remove grime and rust. With a mill bastard file, sharpen the blade's existing bevel.

Insert the new handle, filing or shaving it down if necessary to fit. Hold the tool by the business end, and tap the end of the handle on the ground to drive it into the hasp.

Use an electric drill with a diamond-tip bit to drill a hole through the handle to correspond with the rivet hole in the hasp.

Make a rivet by inserting a pin into the hole, leaving about ¼ inch exposed. Heat the exposed end with a propane torch and strike with a metal hammer to form a rivet head.

Brush linseed oil on the handle to protect it.

HOW TO

Shear Sharpening

Good-quality pruning shears are expensive. But even pricey shears need periodic sharpening and maintenance. Over time, the blades get dull or become nicked, and the works of the shears eventually get gummed up with sap and dirt. Here's how to sharpen and recondition a pair of well-used shears. You'll need a vise to hold the shears while you work, an adjustable wrench, a sturdy knife or screwdriver, a small awl, a wire wheel, a hand drill, a fine-grit diamond file, and grease or other lubricant.

1. Using a wrench, remove the pivot bolt and pry the spring out using a knife or screwdriver.
2. Use an awl or the blade of a small pocketknife to clean out the bolt hole.
3. Lock each handle in a vise and clean the blades using a wire wheel on a hand drill.
4. Sharpen the larger blade using a fine-grit diamond file and making smooth strokes on only the single beveled edge of the blade. (Do not attempt to sharpen the curved blade.)
5. Reassemble, using the bolt and nut
6. Apply lubricant to the blades.
7. Adjust the bolt as necessary for the proper cutting tension.

About 5 percent of air pollution in the United States comes from gas-

powered gardening equipment.

18 The summertime soundtrack of the suburbs includes the swish, swish, swish of sprinkler water that's meant for the grass, splashing onto the sidewalk. The drops quickly sizzle away on the concrete—just one way suburbanites waste water.

Suburban Waterworld. The suburbs are a water wasteland. Much of the H_2O aimed at the lawn and garden runs off and washes away without getting to where plants' roots are waiting. That's because we're not paying attention to our watering hardware.

What to Use Where

Lawn sprinklers: Perfect for lawns, obviously, and large plantings that require occasional water, such as a vegetable garden.

Drip emitters: Trees, shrubs, large plants.

Mini sprinklers: Use for flower and vegetable beds; mass plantings.

There are four basic types of lawn and garden sprinklers that are widely available.

- Stationary sprinklers spray water in a fixed pattern through a small metal or plastic nozzle.
- Oscillating sprinklers throw water through a perforated pipe that sweeps back and forth.
- Revolving sprinklers shoot jets of water in a fixed pattern from rotating arms.
- Impulse or impact sprinklers deliver pulses of water in an adjustable circular pattern.

A Sprinkling of Success. If you choose to use a sprinkler to water your lawn or garden, here's what to look for.

- Uniform coverage. It should deliver the same amount of water at the edge of its throw as it does near the sprinkler.
- Flow rate. A low gallons-per-hour (gph) flow rate is preferred. The slower it flows, the more likely the water is to sink into the ground instead of running off. (You can measure the flow rate of the sprinkler by setting up buckets or other containers at spots

The first lawn sprinkler was patented in 1871.

WISE WATER WAYS

HOW TO

Water Cycling

If your sprinkler seems to waste water no matter how you adjust the pressure from the faucet, that means that the flow rate of the sprinkler exceeds the soil's ability to soak up water. Water infiltration varies tremendously according to soil type. For example, sandy soils can soak up 1 inch of water per hour, while most clay soils will accept only 1/10 inch of water an hour. Rather than buying a new sprinkler, consider water cycling. That means employing a stop-and-go watering method. Run your sprinkler for 15 minutes. Then leave it off for an hour to let the water soak in. Run the sprinkler for another 15-minute period, followed by an hour off. Repeat for a total of 1 hour of sprinkler time. Make it easier on yourself by installing a timer at the faucet to monitor the watering.

around the lawn and measuring the amount of water in the bucket at the end of 1 hour.)
● Throw radius. This is the amount of ground the sprinkler covers with water—the higher the better.

Revolving and stationary sprinklers are the least reliable. Their coverage is uneven, and their throw radius is low. In general, high-quality oscillating and impulse sprinklers offer the best combination of uniform coverage, flow rate, and throw radius.

Do Better with Drip. If you really want to make the most of your water, try dripping instead of sprinkling it on. Developed as an efficient means of watering crops in the deserts of Israel, drip irrigation systems apply tiny amounts of water directly where the plants need it.

Drip irrigation systems save a lot of water. While a typical lawn sprinkler will apply 60 to 300 gallons per hour, a drip mini-sprinkler delivers only 15 gallons per hour, and a drip emitter uses just 1 to 5 gallons per hour. But since that water gets sprinkled or dripped where it's needed, plants get more of what they need, while you apply less.

If you want to give drip irrigation a try, it's best to start with a small kit to get your feet wet, so to speak. That kit should contain the following equipment, along with a customer service number you can call for support, should any complications arise.
● Connections: To hook the system up to your faucet. Hardware required at the water source includes a backflow preventer, a filter, and a pressure regulator.
● Mainline tubing and fittings: 1/2-inch diameter is the most common dimension for the black plastic pipe that carries the water from the source to the garden.
● Stakes: Avoid frustration by securing your tubing.
● Emitters and microsprinklers: Here's the heart of the system. Emitters come in two basic styles: pressure-compensating and noncompensating. The best choice for beginners is pressure-compensating emitters because they provide the same amount of water flow no matter what the water pressure. Compensating emitters can automatically flush themselves out during start up and shutdown. Microspinklers come in all different flow rates and diameters, from the very small to the very large. It's best to have a variety in the system.

• Poly tube punch: For hooking up the emitters and sprinklers along the mainline.

• Goof plugs: Because to err is human.

• Line ends: All good things must end. These plastic plugs close off the system where it ends.

Recycle Your Water.

Every day, 100 gallons or more of slightly used, nearly new water flows from our showers, sinks, and washing machines down our household drains and into the septic system. It seems a waste. And it is, because that water—known as graywater—can be captured and used in the landscape without much difficulty. Not quite sewage but not fresh water either, gray-

water is perfectly safe to reuse as long as you take certain precautions. In fact, there are no reports of anyone in the developed world ever getting sick from properly using graywater.

Graywater Sources. First, identify safe graywater sources. These include water from the bath and shower and from the washing machine, as long as the laundry load does not contain soiled diapers or underwear. Kitchen sink water contains, in part, a sort of "liquid compost" which is, of course, great for the garden. However, this glop can cause great difficulty with some types of graywater hardware. Some authorities have reacted to this by categorically advising against the reuse of kitchen sink

WISE WATER WAYS

water. If you wish to reuse yours, you'll need a special system that's capable of handling it.

A Basic Graywater System. Installing a laundry-only, gravity-flow graywater system is relatively easy. Simply run the drain line from the back of the washing machine out the window, dryer vent, or a small hole drilled in the wall, to a surge tank. The ideal surge tank is a plastic (not metal) 30- or 55-gallon drum with a lid. Install a three-way diverter valve so you can send the graywater to the septic/sewer system if you're washing diapers, or when irrigation is not needed. At the base of the tank, install a male hose adapter. No filtration is needed. Don't put a valve at the outlet, as this creates the possibility of storing graywater, which is not a good idea. From the adapter, you can run the graywater through a ¾-inch garden hose to deep, mulch-filled basins around fruit trees or ornamentals. The hardest part about this simple system is remembering to move the hose: Get in the habit of moving it as part of doing each load of laundry.

TIPS

Where to Use Graywater

You can use graywater on ornamental landscape plants and fruit trees. Avoid applying graywater to vegetable gardens, edible flowers and herbs, and berry bushes.

Rain falling over Europe contains such high

TIPS

Practical Considerations

To avoid accidental ingestion or skin contact, most regulations require subsurface distribution of graywater. Some regulators consider "sub-mulch" to fit the subsurface requirement. From the gardener's standpoint, mulch-filled basins are the ideal way to receive graywater. They contain and cover the flow safely, and they fit in with other horticultural considerations much better than gravel and filter fabric, which have the serious drawback of requiring filtered graywater. Filtration adds complexity to the system and is a big maintenance hassle as well.

If you have to have a completely subsurface graywater system to meet local requirements, a branched-drain graywater system that supplies sub-mulch or sub-soil gravel-less outlet chambers is a good way to go for a small flow.

Always wear rubber or waterproof gloves when dealing with graywater. Check with your local health department to learn about regulations regarding graywater use in your area.

levels of pesticides that it would be illegal to supply it as drinking water.

KEEPING PROBLEMS UNDER CONTROL

Up to 80 million pounds of fungicides are applied annually in the United States.

Some say that the only good bug is a dead bug. However, the billions of dollars spent trying to eradicate every insect have not paid off. Today, farmers lose a greater percentage of their crops to pests than they did 50 years ago.

Got Bugs? Don't Panic; Go Organic.

Like most bumper sticker wisdom, there's some truth to be found in this little rhyme. In short, don't overreact when you see insect pests or their damage to your plants. Big, fat books have been written to describe the many methods of natural pest control. If you have one (or more), by all means, use it. Or follow this short course on the things you really need to know when insects are on the rampage.

Monitor Their Movement. Take the time to find out what's doing the damage and how much real harm it's doing. Go out at various times of day and night (with a magnifying glass and flashlight, if necessary), and stake out the damaged crop to identify the culprit.

Know Your Enemy. Once you've identified the pest, learn about its habits. Will it feed all season, or is this just a temporary phenomenon that you and your garden can withstand? Can you expect future hungry generations? What is the preferred food and feeding time? Which is the best method of organic eradication? On-line gardening sites can provide some of this information, or you can contact your local Cooperative Extension office or check the references in your local library. Make use of the resources you have close at hand, and you may find that the best course of action is no action at all.

Calling All Good Bugs. As with nearly all tasks, you can do the work yourself, or you can get someone (or something) else to do it for you. So, sure, you can spend your time patrolling your garden for pest problems and dealing with them as they occur. Organic gardeners know that a better approach is to keep the local ecosystem in balance, letting the good bugs take care of the bad bugs. You can buy beneficial insects such as lady beetles (a.k.a. ladybugs), lacewings, or mantids from many mail-order catalogs, but that's a stop-gap measure that works best for a confined space, like a greenhouse. It's better to adopt gardening practices that lure a wide variety of beneficial insects to your yard naturally. Make your space attractive to them, and the good guys will set up housekeeping and keep harmful insects under control.

Make Your Yard a Haven for Helpful Insects. First, stop using broad-spectrum pesticides. Right now.

KEEPING PROBLEMS UNDER CONTROL

TIPS

Predators and Their Prey

Here's an overview of some of the garden good guys and the bad bugs they dine upon.

Beneficial Predator	Pests They Prey Upon
Damselfly and dragonfly	Mosquitoes
Spined soldier bug	Mexican bean beetle larvae, Colorado potato beetle larvae, and other beetle grubs
Lacewing	Aphids
Big-eyed bug	Caterpillars, leafhoppers
Damsel bug	Aphids, thrips
Minute pirate bug	Thrips, spider mites, caterpillars
Syrphid fly	Aphids, mealybugs, leafhoppers
Tachinid fly	Japanese beetles, corn borers, grasshoppers
Ground beetle	Aphids, flea beetles

Even the organic ones will kill beneficials along with the pests. Your garden may suffer some short-term losses as the bad bugs temporarily get an upper hand, but as the harmful insect population increases, the beneficial insects will come flying to the rescue, especially if you create a beneficial-friendly habitat.

Shelter. A hedgerow of trees, shrubs, or even fast-growing annuals, such as sunflowers or zinnias, will provide shelter and egg-laying sites for beneficials. A thick layer of mulch is hospitable to ground-dwelling predators, such as ground beetles.

Water. Even a small wading pool or a plant saucer full of water will attract beneficials like damselflies and dragonflies. The downside of keeping a pool of water in the garden is that it will provide a breeding ground for mosquitoes. In a well-balanced system, the 'skeeters will provide food for beneficial insects but, if you'd rather, you can keep them under control with mosquito "donuts" (slow-release *Bacillus thuringiensis* var. *israeliensis*) in the water.

Food. Beneficials don't live on bugs alone. Many, such as tachinid and syrphid flies, subsist on plant nectar and pollen while they wait for pest insects to arrive or hatch. Some plants are especially attractive to beneficials. They include herbs such as caraway, dill, fennel, lemon balm, spearmint, tansy, and other small-flowered plants like buckwheat, clover, cosmos, and Queen-Anne's-lace. Plant them in patches or in rows along the edge of the garden to provide food and shelter for beneficial predators.

Finally, it doesn't pay to be too neat. Many predators and beneficials, including spiders and mantids, are attracted to garden rubbish such as old logs, dried flowerstalks, pallets, rocks, and stones. Leave a little mess to attract them.

Choose Your Poison. In the 1950s, Americans brought better living through chemistry to their suburban backyards, putting pesticides to work on just about any multilegged crawling or flying creature they saw. Spot a bug? Never mind if it's doing any damage—blast it with a spray of insecticide. For the most part, that philosophy still holds. On the average, suburbanites use 10 times more pesticides per area in their yards than farmers do on their fields.

Most folks assume that if you can buy it at the local garden center or hardware store, the stuff is safe. That's a dangerous assumption. In fact, many over-the-counter pesticides are either suspected or known carcinogens, mutagens, or just plain toxins.

Here are some of the more common pesticides you might find in a store, and what they do.

2,4-D is the most widely used herbicide in the world—60 million pounds annually in the United States. It's the weed-killing ingredient found in most weed-and-feed lawn products, and it's also a carcinogen. Two studies by the National Cancer Institute showed an increased incidence of non-Hodgkin's lymphoma among farmers who use 2,4-D. A later NCI study showed that dogs whose owners' lawns were treated with 2,4-D four or more times per year were twice as likely to contract canine malignant lymphoma.

Carbaryl is a popular garden insecticide, widely recommended for controlling Japanese beetles and many other pests of food crops and landscape plants. It is considered moderately to highly toxic, depending upon the formulation of the product in which it's used. Carbaryl affects the central nervous system, and has caused birth defects in laboratory experiments.

Diazinon is a notorious bird killer. Even worse, a study at by the Missouri Department of Health demonstrated that the odds of brain cancer striking children increased by more than four times when their families used diazinon in the garden. This insecticide is a popular choice for controlling ants and beetle grubs in the lawn.

Dichlorvos is a broad-spectrum insecticide found in roach- and ant-control products and many pest strips. One study showed that childhood cancers are three times as likely in homes where pest strips containing dichlorvos were used.

Lindane is an insecticide often found in head-lice shampoos. It's a carcinogen and a suspected mutagen, as well as acutely toxic when inhaled or ingested. Exposure may causes symptoms of apprehension, agitation, vomiting, stomach upset, abdominal pain, and convulsions. The state of California has banned the use of lindane as a treatment for head lice and scabies.

Methoxychlor is an insecticide once sold for mosquito control, among other landscape and garden uses. It damages the reproductive system and nervous system and may cause birth defects.

The evidence is pouring in that regular exposure to all this stuff adds up. Pervasive pesticide use is taking its toll—not so much on the bugs, but on us and our children. A recent study at the University of North Carolina revealed that kids living in homes where the yards were treated with pesticides were four times more likely to be diagnosed with soft tissue sarcomas, compared to kids living where yards were pesticide-free.

Organic Options.

There are plenty of ways to beat lawn and garden pests without resorting to those deadly chemicals. Organic methods include using natural pesticides, traps and barriers, and beneficial insects, such as lady beetles.

There are several classes of natural pesticides. Some are more effective than others; some are more dangerous. Just because these products are natural or plant-derived, they're not necessarily totally safe. Many are broad-spectrum insecticides, which means they kill any insects they contact, including beneficials.

Botanical Pesticides. Derived from plants, botanical pesticides offer certain advantages over petrochemical-based products. The main benefit of choosing a botanical pesticide is that these products don't linger long in the environment. Where synthetic sprays and dusts may persist for months—or even years—botanicals break down to harmless compounds, usually within days. Still, these are pesticides, and they may harm organisms other than the pest that's giving you problems. Choose them only as a last resort, and follow the label directions carefully.

Pyrethrin is made from the dried, powdered flowers of the pyrethrum daisy (*Tanacetum cinerariifolium* and *T. coccineum*). This is the most commonly used organic insecticide. Pyrethrin is used as a spray or dust and is known for its quick action against virtually all insect pests. Pyrethrin degrades rapidly and is nontoxic to humans. Avoid confusing pyrethrin products with synthetic pesticides that contain "pyrethroids."

Neem is derived from the seeds of the neem tree (*Azadirachta indica*), a shade tree that's native to the Indian subcontinent. Applied as a spray, neem works against pests in several ways, acting as a repellent or feeding deterrent, as a growth hormone interrupter, and as a toxin when insects eat it. This makes neem effective against many different pests, yet it has very low toxicity to humans and other mammals.

Basic Pest Control Methods

If it turns out that the pest in question is a serious threat to your garden or landscape, here's a list of safe, sane, and effective options for dealing with the problem.

Trap 'em. You can catch your fair share of pests using slug traps (yes, beer makes a fine bait), sticky yellow cards for whiteflies and aphids, Japanese beetle traps (locate them far from beetles' favorite plants), and others.

Pick 'em. Big, slow pests are easy pickings. You can grab them (wear gloves if you're squeamish) and dispose of them by drowning, smashing, or some other creative means. Cutworms, other caterpillars, and tomato hornworms are all pickable. So are slugs, if you like to garden after dark.

Block 'em. Keep pests away from plants using barriers of cardboard (cutworm collars around young transplants), Reemay (spunbonded floating row covers over plants), sticky goop (Tanglefoot circling tree trunks), and paper bags covering fruit on trees.

Hose 'em. Small, soft-bodied pests, such as aphids, are easily washed from your plants with a strong spray of water from the hose. The water also helps wash away the sticky "honeydew" the aphids leave behind, and the ants that subsequently show up to feast on it.

Spray or dust 'em. If you're into the spray-and-pray method of pest control, you can find an organic alternative spray or dust to take care of any pest—*as a last resort*. Read on for information on some of the safest options (see page 144), check an organic pest control manual, or read the labels at your full-service garden center.

Resist 'em. Some plants, especially turfgrasses and trees, resist damage from certain widespread pests. Research a specific plant's resistance before you buy.

Oils, Soaps, and Others. Not every pesticide available to organic gardeners comes from plants. Many horticultural oils are derived from petroleum, although vegetable oil–based sprays are becoming more widely available; they work by coating and suffocating soft-bodied pests during almost any stage of their life cycle. Orchardists have used dormant oils to control pests for decades. Now, a new generation of super-fine grade oil can be used year-round in the home garden. Oil sprays are most effective against mites, whiteflies, and scale. They're very nontoxic to mammals and have no lingering residual effect. New oil products, made with vegetable oils, on the market may be even more environmentally benign. One such spray combines canola oil with pyrethrin.

Horticultural soaps are an old home remedy that has gone mainstream. Now, you can buy insecticidal soaps that are specially formulated to avoid injury to

Pesticides from Plants

Plant-derived botanical pesticides occupied gardeners' pest-fighting arsenals long before chemical pesticides were invented. You may be familiar with one of the oldest, an extremely effective pest-killer called nicotine, which was derived from tobacco plants. In spite of its apparently benign origins, nicotine (sold as nicotine sulfate) was recognized as a powerful poison long before the chemical products sitting next to it on the shelf earned similar attention. Most of the botanical pesticides available today are much less toxic than nicotine, but these products still pose risks that should not be ignored. While switching from chemical pesticides to botanical controls is a step in the right direction, it's not the final step en route to a safe, healthy home landscape.

Ultimately, your goal should be a garden that doesn't need sprays or dusts—even botanical ones—to keep pests at bay. After all, if you're gardening to grow fresh, pesticide-free food for your family, it makes little sense to put poisons of any kind on your plants.

plants. Soaps act quickly, have no residual effect, and are effective against many pests, especially small, soft-bodied insects such as aphids, leafhoppers, and spider mites.

Microbial pesticides are powders or liquids derived from naturally occurring soil microbes. These are among the newest and most effective organic controls. They include BT, or *Bacillus thurengiensis*, a product that's in the news lately because it is being genetically engineered into many, many crops, much to the chagrin of organic activists who predict dire consequences (including pest resistance). As it is, BT is a perfect pesticide because it is highly specific and kills only target pests. It works quickly—pests often stop feeding immediately upon ingesting BT and die within days. BT offers some residual control, but it does not persist in the environment. There are now several strains available that will kill gypsy moths, hornworms, cabbageworms, cutworms, corn borers, and even mosquitoes.

Another important and popular microbial insecticide is milky disease spore, *Bacillus popilliae*. This powder is used to control Japanese beetle grubs. Sprinkled on the lawn in early summer, it gradually colonizes a lawn and kills any grubs that eat it.

Get Physical. Sprays and dusts seem like magical pest-stopping elixirs, but they have their down sides, too. To garden with no fear of any kind of poison on your plants, go with physical controls that either remove pests from your plants or stop them from reaching your garden in the first place.

Hand-picking. Large, slow-moving pests such as slugs, tomato hornworms, and some beetles can be eliminated by hand (if handling them doesn't creep you out too much.). Hunt them down in the morning when they are sluggish, and do them in however you like.

Row covers. Sheer, see-through row covers made of spun-bonded polyester can seal a garden bed against marauding pests while still allowing sun and water to

KEEPING PROBLEMS UNDER CONTROL

get through. They're best used early in the year on vegetable gardens to keep out flea beetles, cucumber beetles, maggot flies, and cabbage loopers.

Collars and wraps. Slug barriers made of copper keep the creepy things from passing. Cardboard collars protect young seedlings from cutworms. Sticky tree wraps will keep some pests, like gypsy moth larvae, from climbing trees to munch on the leaves.

Traps. Sticky yellow traps snare aphids, thrips, and whiteflies. They're especially effective indoors or in a greenhouse. To create your own, paint a square of wood or plastic bright yellow (like Rustoleum safety yellow) and coat it with Tanglefoot. Hang the coated trap within 1 foot of susceptible plants.

Slugs are attracted to the scent of alcohol and fermented grain. In other words, they love beer. Take advantage of their taste for brews by filling a small dish or empty tuna or cat food can with beer, and place it so its rim is flush with the soil surface. They'll creep in, drink their fill, and never creep out. Check every morning, and remove drunk and drowned slugs.

Most important of all: Be patient and use discretion. Don't reach for a pesticide every time you see a bug, and don't act until you see real damage.

About 70 million pounds of pesticides are applied to U.S. home lawns and gardens annually.

Disease Prevention.

Yellow spots on the leaves. Rot on the fruit. White powdery stuff everywhere. Surely there's something you can spray, right? Think again. Diseases on plants are harder to cure than the common cold and, like most cold medications, the sprays you can use tend to treat the disease symptoms rather than the cause of the problem. Besides, the only "fun" in fungicides is in the spelling. These chemicals are downright dangerous. Save yourself a lot of trouble, time, and exposure to poisons by eliminating garden conditions that contribute to disease problems in the first place.

- **Give 'em air.** Poor air circulation around plants allows excess moisture and dew to linger, creating the continuously wet conditions where disease organisms thrive. Trim trees and shrubs to open dead air pockets.
- **Water properly.** Don't water late in the evening when moisture is likely to remain on the leaves all night, fostering disease.
- **Mulch.** Spores of many diseases, such as tomato blight, reside in the soil. When rain falls, the spores can splash up and infect the plant. You can stop that cycle by mulching plants with a natural mulch like straw. A layer of compost works even better because it contains microorganisms that compete against the fungus before it has a chance to spread onto the leaves.
- **Again, resist 'em.** There are many, many cultivars of ornamental and food plants that resist disease. Find out which diseases are problems in your area, and shop for cultivars that resist those specific ailments.
- **Clean it up.** Disease organisms also linger in garden refuse. Clean up old plants and debris at the end of the year and dispose of them properly.

Weed 'Em and Reap.

Multilegged critters and microscopic fungi are not the only pests that will try to take over your garden. Pest plants will show up, too. Some of them will seem to move as quickly as those problems that arrive on wings or legs. The key to weed control is to keep ahead of them—and to keep your head if you fall behind. Don't lose sight of your goal to have a landscape that's healthy and organic, and don't let a lawn laced with dandelions drive you into dumping several bags full of toxins onto the grass where your kids play and your dog rolls.

There's a place in New Jersey where grass is the weed, and farmers work hard to keep it out of their dandelion fields. It just goes to show you that weeds are a matter of perspective. In fact many turf "weeds," such as viola, creeping Charley, and speedwell, originally were imported as ornamentals.

Still, there are some plants that are just plain noxious weeds, no matter how charitable you're feeling. They have to go, but that doesn't mean reaching for an herbicide. There are several nontoxic ways to wipe them out

Mulch Ado. Weeds need air, water, and light to grow. Deprive them of any of those elements, especially the last, and eventually they will be foiled. That's the principle behind mulch, as it covers the soil to keep the weeds from germinating. There are several different types of mulch available, each with advantages and disadvantages, depending on where you want to use it.

Organic mulches, such as straw, compost, or grass clippings, are most desirable because they let water penetrate into the soil while adding nutrients and improving soil tilth as they decompose. Organic mulch does have to be replenished as it breaks down, and some types may contain weed seeds. Newspaper is a free mulch that earthworms love. It also improves the soil and lets water reach plants' roots. Unfortunately, it's not very attractive, so it's usually covered with a more attractive mulch layer. And it's hard to work with in the wind.

Petrochemical-derived mulches like black plastic and landscape fabric do a great job of stopping weeds, but only until they start to tear and deteriorate. Then, weeds quickly pop up in the gaps, and the plastic becomes a mess for you to get out of your garden. They're also unattractive and have to be hidden beneath more decorative mulches.

Natural-Born Weed Killers. Until recently, all of the quick-fix herbicides were derived from synthetic chemicals. Most had toxic and long-lasting effects on soil and human health. These days, though, there are a couple of natural, perfectly safe, and effective organic alternatives.

Safer's Sharpshooter, a product made from fatty acids, is a broad-spectrum herbicide that kills all vegetation on contact. Well, on contact is a bit of an exaggeration. It may require repeated spraying to kill old, established, and tough weeds.

Corn gluten meal is a totally safe pre-emergent herbicide. (See page 102 for more information.)

Burn, Baby, Burn. Years ago, before the advent of chemicals such as methyl bromide, farmers used heat to sterilize soil and kill weed seeds. In those days, the heat was provided by gas burners. These days you can use the sun's heat to sterilize soil. It's called solarization, and here's how to do it.

1. Till or spade a garden bed and rake it smooth, removing all rocks, stones, and soil clumps.

2. Water the bed until it is thoroughly moist to a depth of 6 inches.

3. Cover the bed tightly with a sheet of 2- to 4-mil clear plastic, anchoring the plastic around the edges with soil.

4. Leave the plastic on for at least 6 to 8 weeks during the hottest times of summer.

5. Remove the plastic and plant. Enrich the newly solarized soil with compost to replace soil organisms that perished along with the weed seeds.

Hoe, Hoe, Hoe. At some point, weed control comes down to elbow grease. You're going to have to hoe, chop, and physically remove those weeds. Here are some of the best tools for doing the job.

- A good field hoe or onion hoe for open-ground weed removal
- A mattock for tough, deep-rooted weeds
- An asparagus knife to cut off weed roots beneath the soil surface
- A Cape Cod weeder for hand-weeding in beds and other tight spots
- A crack weeder for clearing weeds from walkways and tight corners in garden beds
- A dandelion weeder for digging out weeds with long taproots
- A sharp-bladed collinear hoe or diamond-shaped hoe for removing small weeds in close quarters
- A pair of sturdy gloves to protect your hands

Recommended Reading

Benjamin, Joan, and Deborah L. Martin, eds. *Great Garden Formulas*. Emmaus, PA: Rodale, 1998.

Brower, Michael, and Warren Leon. *The Consumer's Guide to Effective Environmental Choices: Practical Advice from the Union of Concerned Scientists*. New York: Three Rivers Press, 1999.

Claflin, Edward, ed. *The Experts Book of Hints, Tips & Everyday Wisdom*. Emmaus, PA: Rodale, 1993.

Creasy, Rosalind. *The Complete Book of Edible Landscaping*. San Francisco, CA: Sierra Club, 1982.

Dadd-Redalia, Debra. *Sustaining the Earth: Choosing Consumer Products That Are Safe for You, Your Family, and the Earth*. New York: Hearst Books, 1994.

Editors of Rodale Organic Gardening Magazine and Books. *Rodale Organic Gardening Basics: Lawns*. Emmaus, PA: Rodale, 2000.

Editors of Rodale Organic Gardening Magazine and Books. *Rodale Organic Gardening Basics: Soil*. Emmaus, PA: Rodale, 2000.

Editors of Rodale Organic Gardening Magazine and Books. *Rodale Organic Gardening Basics: Vegetables*. Emmaus, PA: Rodale, 2000.

Kourik, Robert. *Drip Irrigation for Every Landscape and All Climates: Helping Your Garden Flourish, While Conserving Water!* Santa Rosa, CA: Metamorphic Press, 1992.

Ludwig, Art. *Create an Oasis with Greywater.* Santa Barbara, CA: Oasis Design, 2000.

Ogden, Shepherd. *Straight-Ahead Organic: A Step-by-Step Guide to Growing Great Vegetables in a Less-Than-Perfect World*. White River Junction, VT: Chelsea Green, 1999.

Organic Gardening magazine. Rodale, 33 E. Minor Street, Emmaus, PA 18098.

Roth, Sally. *Natural Landscaping: Gardening with Nature to Create a Backyard Paradise*. Emmaus, PA: Rodale, 1997.

Schultz, Warren. *A Man's Turf: The Perfect Lawn*. New York: Clarkson Potter, 1999.

Resources

Turn to the businesses and organizations listed here to find sources for the products and materials mentioned in this book. These listings also include Web sites that offer additional information about some of the topics addressed. Be a wise consumer of Internet information: Sites that end in ".com" sell goods and services along with any information they provide. A site that ends with ".org" or ".gov" may be less commercial in content, but not necessarily less biased toward a particular point of view.

Garden Products

Seeds & Plants

W. Atlee Burpee
300 Park Avenue
Warminster, PA 18974
Phone: (800) 888-1447
Fax: (215) 674-4170
Web site: www.burpee.com
Large selection of seeds and plants of annuals, perennials, vegetables, and herbs

The Cook's Garden
P.O. Box 535
Londonderry, VT 05148
Phone: (800) 457-9703
Fax: (800) 457-9705
Web site: www.cooksgarden.com
Seeds and supplies for the kitchen gardener

Forestfarm
990 Tetherow Road
Williams, OR 97544-9599
Phone: (541) 846-7269
Fax: (541) 846-6963
Web site: www.forestfarm.com
Large collection of ornamental plants, including many American natives

Johnny's Selected Seeds
Foss Hill Road
Albion, ME 04910
Phone: (207) 437-4357
Fax: (800) 437-4290
Web site: www.johnnyseeds.com
Vegetable, herb, and flower seeds; also tools, organic fertilizers, and pest control products

Niche Gardens
1111 Dawson Road
Chapel Hill, NC 27516
Phone: (919) 967-0078
Web site: www.nichegdn.com
Nursery-propagated wildflowers and perennials

Pinetree Garden Seeds
P.O. Box 300
New Gloucester, ME 04260
Phone: (207) 926-3400
Fax: (888) 527-3337
Web site: www.superseeds.com
Specializes in small packets of vegetable, herb, and flower seeds at reduced prices

Prairie Nursery
P.O. Box 306
Westfield, WI 53964
Phone: (800) 476-9453
Fax: (608) 296-2741
Web site: www.prairienursery.com
Native prairie, wetland, and woodland wildflowers, grasses, and sedges

Territorial Seed Co.
P.O. Box 157
Cottage Grove, OR 97424
Phone: (541) 942-9547
Fax: (888) 657-3131
Web site: www.territorial-seed.com
Seed selected for short seasons and cool climates

Wildginger Woodlands
P.O. Box 1091
Webster, NY 14580
Northeastern wildflowers and ferns

Drip Irrigation Supplies

The Drip Store
395 North Hale Avenue
Escondido, Calif. 92029
Phone: (760) 735-3225
Fax: (760) 735-3255
Web site: www.dripirrigation.com

Rain Bird Sprinkler Mfg. Corp.
145 North Grand Avenue
Glendora, CA 91741-2469
Phone: (626) 963-9311
Web site: www.rainbird.com

Tools, Organic Fertilizers & Pest-Control Products

A. M. Leonard, Inc.
241 Fox Drive
P.O. Box 816
Piqua, OH 45356-0816
Phone: (800) 543-8955
Fax: (800) 433-0633
Web site: www.amleo.com
Large selection of tools

Biosensory, Inc.
Windham Mills Technology Center
322 Main Street
Building 1, 2nd floor
Willimantic, CT 06226-3149
Phone: (860) 423-3009
Fax: (860) 423-3028
Web site: www.biosensory.com
Manufacturers of the Dragonfly mosquito eater

Gardens Alive!
5100 Schenley Place
Lawrenceburg, IN 47025
Phone: (812) 537-8651
Fax: (812) 537-5108
Web site: www.gardens-alive.com
Complete selection of organic fertilizers and pest controls, corn gluten meal for weed control, and also natural pet care products

Gardener's Supply Company
128 Intervale Road
Burlington, VT 05401
Phone: (888) 833-1412
Fax: (800) 551-6712
Web site: www.gardeners.com
Organic fertilizers and pest control; also tools, seed starting supplies, and home products

Peaceful Valley Farm Supply
P.O. Box 2209
Grass Valley, CA 95945
Phone: (888) 784-1722
Fax: (530) 272-4794
Web site: www.groworganic.com
Tools, seeds, fertilizers, and pest controls for organic gardeners; also natural pet care products

Smith and Hawken
P.O. Box 6900
Florence, KY 41022-6900
Phone: (800) 940-1170
Fax: (606) 727-1166
Web site: www.smith-hawken.com
Garden tools and related products

Home Care Information & Products

Center for Neighborhood Technology
2125 W. North Avenue
Chicago, IL 60647
Phone: (773) 278-4800
Web site: www.cnt.org/wetcleaning/
Information about less-toxic alternatives for dry cleaning clothes, including where to find an environmentally conscious cleaner in your region

Chemical Specialties, Inc.
One Woodlawn Green, Suite 250
200 East Woodlawn Road
Charlotte, NC 28217
Phone: (800) 421-8661
Fax: (704) 527-8232
Web site: www.treatedwood.com/consumer/
    preserveplus.html
Preserve Plus brand arsenic-free treated wood

Harmony
360 Interlocken Boulevard, Suite 300
Broomfield, CO 80021
Phone: (303) 464-3600
Fax: (303) 464-3700
Web site: www.gaiam.com
Products for environmentally conscious consumers

Healthy Home Center
1403-A Cleveland Street
Clearwater, FL 33755
Phone: (727) 447-4454
Fax: (727) 447-0140
Web site: www.healthyhome.com
A complete line of nontoxic products

Interlock Paving Systems, Inc.
802 West Pembroke Avenue
Hampton, VA 23699
Phone: (800) 572-3189
Fax: (757) 723-8895
Web site: www.interlockonline.com/environ.html
Permeable, interlocking driveway stones

Real Goods
200 Clara Avenue
Ukiah, CA 95482-4004
Phone: (800) 762-7325
Fax: (800) 508-2342
Web site: www.realgoods.com
Healthy home products

Seventh Generation
One Mill Street
Burlington, VT 05401-1530
Phone: (802) 658-3773
Fax: (802) 658-1771
Web site: www.seventhgen.com
Ecological cleaning and paper products

RESOURCES

U.S. Department of Energy, Energy Star Program
Phone: (888) STAR YES (782-7937)
Web site: www.energystar.gov
The Environmental Protection Agency's guide to the household appliances that use the least amount of electricity and/or water

Environmental Information

American Council for an Energy-Efficient Economy
1001 Connecticut Avenue, NW
Suite 801
Washington, DC 20036
Research and Conferences: (202) 429-8873
Publications: (202) 429-0063
Web site: www.aceee.org
A nonprofit organization dedicated to advancing energy efficiency as a means of promoting both economic prosperity and environmental protection

Environmental Defense Fund
Environmental Defense National Headquarters
257 Park Avenue S
New York, NY 10010
Phone: (212) 505-2100
Fax: (212) 505-2375
Web site: www.environmentaldefense.org
A nonprofit organization dedicated to protecting the environment. Among their many informative Web site offerings is Green Car: A Guide to Cleaner Vehicle Production, Use, and Disposal.

Environmental Working Group
1718 Connecticut Avenue NW
Suite 600
Washington, DC 20009
Phone: (202) 667-6982
Fax: (202) 232-2592
Web site: www.ewg.org
Cutting-edge articles and reports about health and environmental issues

U.S. Department of Energy Fuel Economy Site
9300 Lee Highway
Fairfax, VA 22031
Phone: (800) 423-1363
Web site: www.fueleconomy.gov/feg/index.htm
Compares gas mileage, fuel costs, and emissions of new and used vehicles

Pesticides

National Coalition Against the Misuse of Pesticides
701 E Street SE
Suite 200
Washington, DC 20003
Phone: (202) 543-5450
Fax: (202) 543-4791
Web site: www.beyondpesticides.org
Information about pesticides and alternatives to their use

Northwest Coalition for Alternatives to Pesticides
P.O. Box 1393
Eugene, OR 97440
Phone: (541) 344-5044
Fax: (541) 344-6923
Web site: www.pesticide.org
Reports and fact sheets about pesticides in the environment and their alternatives

U.S. Environmental Protection Agency
Office of Pesticide Programs
Ariel Rios Building
1200 Pennsylvania Avenue NW
Washington, DC 20460
Web site: www.epa.gov/pesticides
U.S. government reports and information about pesticides

Photo Credits

Index

INDEX